Through the Eyes of the Disciple Jesus Loved

Thru The First Disciple's Eyes, Volume 2

John H Brennan

Published by John H Brennan, 2023.

THROUGH THE EYES OF THE DISCIPLE JESUS LOVED

First edition. May 30, 2023.

Copyright © 2023 John H Brennan.

ISBN: 979-8223375104

Written by John H Brennan.

Table of Contents

To my beautiful wife, Theresa for her unwavering support of
my own faith journey.

Introduction

Between the covers of this book, I attempt to take you on a journey through the eyes of the disciple that Jesus loved. Not wanting to quote scripture, but to fill in the blanks of scripture. To help you see what John saw. To hear what John heard. To feel what John felt.

You will begin this journey on Golgotha as John had to not only deal with his own grief, but also console the Blessed Mother Mary. Then to the tomb, and on to the upper room to wait and cry and wonder, when will they come for us? Three days pass and the Lord rises from the dead! Even with the new strength from the knowledge of the Resurrection, we hide in the locked room, then He appears to us! The second time he appears, Thomas is there, having not believed that we saw and talked with the Risen Christ. Jesus invites Thomas to put his fingers in the nail holes in His hands and feet and his hand into his side. Then Jesus asks for something to eat!

A month passes and Jesus leads you and the others out to the vicinity of Bethany, which is situated on the eastern slope of the Mount of Olives, a half a day's hike! There, He says that He will send an advocate who will always be with us and remind us all He said and did. Then blessed us all and floated into the sky. Then two men in white robes appeared and said "Why do you stand here looking into the sky?" We all feel foolish as this implies a gentle reminder to us that our task and focus should not be solely on the sight of Jesus ascending, but on the mission He had entrusted to us.

The journey continues with the daunting task of preaching the Good News to all and more personally, the task of keeping Mother Mary safe from all harm, even if it takes bringing her to a safe city far away.

Enjoy the images and dialog John may have had with the other Apostles, Mary and those he ministered to.

If you like this type of book, please return to the book seller's web page and rate it so that I will be encouraged to write more of what the Holy Spirit tells me to.

At the Cross

I stand at the foot of the cross, my heart pounding in my chest as I witness the excruciating agony that my beloved friend and savior, Jesus, is enduring. My eyes are fixed on him, unable to look away from the horrific scene that is unfolding before me.

Only a week ago, we had been in Jerusalem, celebrating Jesus' arrival as the welcome savior and king of the Jews. The crowds had lined the streets, waving palm branches and shouting praises. We had felt so hopeful and full of joy, certain that our Lord would finally triumph over all adversity.

But now, that same triumphant King is writhing in agony before me, hanging from a cross like a common criminal. The memory of that joyous day seems like a cruel joke, mocking our faith and hope in the face of such unspeakable suffering.

I look around and see Mary, the Mother of Jesus; Salome, his mother's sister who was the mother of James the little and Joses; Mary the wife of Cleophas; and Mary Magdalene, their faces twisted in grief and despair.

Standing at a distance were a large number of people who had followed him, including women who mourned and wailed for him on the way and several who knew him, including the women who had followed him from Galilee, But I cannot shed tears. The anguish inside me is too raw, too visceral. I am numb, my heart shattered into a million pieces as I watch Jesus suffer.

As I stand back and gaze upon that chaotic and overwhelming scene, I take in the horde of people gathered at a distance. Among the throngs, I see the women, their tears flowing freely as they weep for the beloved son, brother, and friend who hangs before them. I see the soldiers, standing at attention but unable to hide the looks of shock and disbelief etched upon their faces. I see the scoundrels, who had been crucified alongside Jesus, writhing in agony and crying out in pain.

And yet, amidst all this chaos and pain, there is something almost sacred about the scene. I see the centurion, his armor glinting in the sun, gazing up at the Cross with a look of reverence and awe. I see the chief priests, their faces contorted with anger and frustration as they realize that they have failed to silence the man they saw as a threat to their power. I see the members of the Sanhedrin, many of them wringing their hands and muttering to themselves, struggling to comprehend the enormity of what is happening before them.

But perhaps most striking of all is the vast crowd of people from all walks of life who have come to witness the crucifixion. They are a microcosm of humanity, each one representing a different aspect of the human experience. There are the wealthy and powerful, looking down from their lofty perches with a mix of curiosity and disdain. There are the poor and downtrodden, their faces etched with pain and suffering as they see one of their own suffering on the Cross. There are the sinners and the saints, the lost and the found, the broken and the whole. All of them have been drawn to this place, to witness the ultimate sacrifice of a man who had come to offer them hope and redemption.

I temporarily lose myself in a prophetic vision of all the people who would be drawn to the Cross in the centuries to come. I see the young and the old, the rich and the poor, the powerful and the powerless. We see people of every race, every language, every culture, all of them gathered around the Cross, drawn by the promise of salvation and the hope of a new life.

Then I return my gaze upon this scene; I cannot help but be moved by the sheer magnitude of what is happening before us. I see in this moment the culmination of all the hopes and dreams of generations past and future, the ultimate sacrifice that would offer humanity the chance to be reconciled with their Creator. I see the profound love that drove Jesus to the Cross, and I feel the weight of our own sin and brokenness as I stand before it.

I look at Mary, his mother, standing beside me. She's weeping uncontrollably, her body shaking with sobs. I take Mary's hand, and I feel her warmth. And suddenly, I know what I have to do. I have to be strong for her. I have to be the rock she can lean on when everything else is falling apart.

I turn back to Jesus, and I watch as he struggles for breath. The sky has grown dark, and the air is thick with the scent of blood and sweat. I feel sick to my stomach, but I can't leave. I can't look away.

And then, in the midst of it all, he speaks. "Woman, behold thy son," he says, motioning towards me. My heart stops for a moment as I realize what he means. He is entrusting his mother, Mary, to my care. The responsibility is overwhelming, but I know I must do all that I can to protect her and honor Jesus' wishes.

And then I realize what Jesus has done. He's given me his mother to care for. It's an honor, but it's also a burden. How can I care for her when my own heart is breaking into a million pieces?

As I hold Mary's hand, I am struck by a flood of memories. Memories of the countless moments of kindness and compassion that Jesus had shown to me, and the deep bond of friendship that we had shared. I think of all the times that he had comforted and healed the sick, the broken-hearted, and the outcast. And now, as I stand here watching him suffer, I am filled with a sense of overwhelming gratitude for all that he has done for us.

But there is also fear, as I realize the danger that we are in. The Jewish leaders and the Roman soldiers are watching us closely, looking for any opportunity to silence us and quash the message of love and hope that Jesus had come to spread. I am here not only to comfort Mary, but also to protect her from harm.

As Jesus' breathing becomes more labored and his strength begins to fade, I can feel my own strength failing me. The darkness of the sky and the rumble of thunder overhead seem to reflect the storm of emotions swirling inside me. And then, with his last breath, he utters the words that will forever change the course of history: "It is finished."

For a moment, we stood in silence, each lost in our own thoughts and emotions. I looked to Mary and saw the pain etched deep in her eyes as she lovingly kissed her son's bloody feet and wailed in emotional agony. She knew that his death was required to show that generation and all future generations the depth of his love, forgiveness and desire for them to live a life like his, loving all and forgiving all so that they would be worthy of eternal life with him in heaven.

One of the soldiers stepped forward with a spear and thrust it into Jesus' side, piercing his heart. Blood and water sprayed from his side, an image which would last until the end of the earth as a testament to the immense Love and Forgiveness that Jesus had shown us all, even in his darkest hour. This memory will sear into my mind like a branding iron. It will remind me of the pain and sorrow that Mary endured, the weight of her loss - too much for anyone to bear.

Joseph of Arimathea ran up the hill of Golgotha, his heart racing with urgency as he clutched a decree from Pilate in his hand. The Roman governor had granted him permission to take down the body of Jesus from the cross and give him a proper burial.

As he approached the top of the hill, Joseph could see the soldiers standing guard around the three crosses that had been erected on the hilltop. He took a deep breath and approached them, his heart heavy with sorrow at the sight of his friend and savior, Jesus, hanging lifelessly from the center cross.

"Soldiers," Joseph said, his voice shaking with emotion. "I have come to take down the body of Jesus for burial. I have the governor's decree here."

The soldiers eyed him suspiciously, but after seeing the official seal on the decree, they reluctantly agreed to comply with Joseph's request. Joseph climbed up the ladder to reach Jesus, carefully holding his body with cloth strips as the soldiers removed the spiked nails, throwing them one by one to the ground and laughing that Jesus couldn't remove them himself. It was agonizing to watch as the soldiers pounded the nails out of Jesus' hands and feet. I did our best to shield Mary from the sight, but it was clear that the memory of her son's suffering would haunt her for the rest of her days.

Finally, the soldiers finished their work, and Joseph and the soldiers carefully lowered Jesus' limp body down from the cross and lays Him down with His mother. Mary sits on the ground below the cross, cradling Jesus' body and rocking it gently back and forth. Her sobs are almost too much to bear, the raw emotion and pain etched on her face. But in that moment, she is also proud, proud of what her son has done for all of humanity.

As we carry Jesus' body toward the tomb, I am struck by the finality of it all. My friend, my teacher, my savior, is gone. But even as we mourn his passing, we know that his legacy will live on, that his message of love and forgiveness will continue to inspire generations to come. It was a solemn procession filled with sorrow and grief. The sky was now dark and foreboding, the air filled with an eerie stillness that only deepened our sense of loss.

Once the tomb was in sight, we could see the Roman guards standing at the entrance, their swords ready. Joseph approached them and handed over the decree from Pilate, and after a brief inspection, they stepped aside and allowed us to enter.

But Joseph and I paid them no heed, focused only on honoring Jesus' memory and preparing him for burial. We carried his body to the anointing stone, where we all washed him and anointed him with spices and perfumed oils, the sweet scent of the oils mingling with the salty tang of our tears.

Carefully, we wrapped his body in the burial cloth, as if we were cradling him in our arms one last time. It was a tender moment, filled with love and reverence, as we prepared to lay him to rest. It is a small comfort, but one that we cling to, a way to show our love and respect for the man who gave so much to us.

We laid Jesus' body on the stone shelf, taking care to arrange him in a position of rest and peace. It was difficult to believe that the man who had healed the sick, fed the hungry, and preached messages of love and hope to the masses was now gone. After a quiet and somber moment, we said our final goodbyes. The stone is rolled over the entrance, sealing it shut. It is a heavy, final sound, one that will echo through my soul for years to come.

The soldiers standing guard watched as we disappeared into the evening sky. Joseph knew the way back to his house where we would gather in the upper room to rest and console each other.

Waiting in the Upper Room

As I arrived at the upper room with Mary, the weight of grief and despair settled heavily on my heart. The group of disciples and apostles had already gathered, and tears were streaming down their faces. Peter, James, and Andrew were huddled together, their shoulders shaking with sobs. Thomas sat alone in a corner; his head bowed in anguish.

Mary clung to my arm; her body wracked with sobs. I tried to offer her words of comfort, but my own sorrow was so great that my words came out of my mouth all jumbled, not making much sense.

We all wept bitterly, each of us mourning the loss of our beloved Teacher and friend. For hours, we cried out in anguish, unable to console each other or find any solace in our tears.

As the night wore on, we turned to prayer, seeking comfort and guidance from God. We prayed for strength to endure the pain of our loss and for understanding of what was to come. Our voices mingled together in a desperate plea for help and mercy.

In the midst of our grief, we also shared our memories of Jesus, talked about the events that led up to his death, and debated the significance of his teachings and miracles. We sought to make sense of what had happened, to understand why our Lord had been taken from us.

Mary, the mother of Jesus, was devastated by the loss of her son, and the group rallied around her, offering words of comfort and support. We held her close, embracing her and sharing in her pain.

Despite our sorrow, we still needed to eat, and we gathered around a table to share meals and break bread together, as He taught us the night before. We ate in silence, our hearts heavy with grief and our minds filled with memories of Jesus.

In moments of silence and reflection, we also sang hymns of praise and worship, lifting our voices in gratitude for the time we had spent with Jesus. We sang of his love, his mercy, and his grace, and we were comforted by the knowledge that he was with us, even in death.

We poured over the scriptures, searching for answers and insights into what had happened and what was to come. We studied the prophecies of the Messiah in the Old Testament, seeking to understand how they had been fulfilled in Jesus.

Mary recounted the discussion she had with Simeon after Jesus' circumcision, "I remember the day that Simeon came to see us. He was an old man, but there was something about him that made me feel like he had seen and done things that no one else had. He had heard about our baby, and he said that he had been waiting to see him for a long time. I didn't really understand what he meant, but I could tell that he was excited."

She continued, "When he saw Jesus, he took him in his arms and held him close. He looked up to the sky and thanked God for letting him see this day. I was touched by his words, but also a little bit confused. Why was he so emotional about my baby?"

"But then, he said something that made my heart skip a beat. He said that Jesus was destined for greatness, but that his life would also be full of sorrow and pain. I felt a lump form in my throat as I realized what he was saying. My baby, my precious son, was going to suffer." Mary shared.

With tears rolling down her cheeks, she said "As Simeon continued to speak, his words grew more and more ominous. He said that Jesus would be a sign of contradiction, that many would reject him, and that even my own soul would be pierced by a sword. I didn't want to believe him, but I knew deep down that he was speaking the truth, as Gabriel told me months earlier."

Mary choked back more tears and said "In that moment, I felt a sense of fear and sadness wash over me. I knew that my life, and the life of my son, would never be the same again. But even in the face of this uncertainty, I knew that God was with us, and that he had a plan for our lives. So I held my baby close, and I prayed that God would give us the strength and courage to face whatever lay ahead. Now I know."

Peter gathered us all together for evening prayers knowing the level of physical, emotional and spiritual exhaustion they all had. Peter began the prayer "Our Lord and Savior, we come to you broken and humbled, in the midst of our deepest sorrow and despair. We have witnessed the unimaginable, as you were taken from us and crucified before our very eyes.

We have seen the darkness that has descended upon this world, as the forces of evil seemed to triumph over goodness and light. We have felt the weight of our own doubts and fears, as we wondered if all that we believed in was nothing but a dream.

But now, we gather in this upper room, seeking solace and strength in your presence. We know that you have promised to rise again, and we cling to that hope with all that we have.

Please, Lord, grant us the courage to face the trials that lie ahead. Give us the wisdom to understand your teachings, and the strength to follow them even when it seems impossible. And most of all, help us to hold fast to the faith that you have instilled in us, no matter what trials or tribulations may come.

We ask for your mercy and your grace, and we place our trust in your unfailing love. Amen."

The next morning, the sun began to shine brightly thru the windows and the birds were singing their sweet melodies. I hoped that this would set the tone for the day after a couple of long and devastating days for all of us.

The group discussed what we should do next. We talked about how we could spread the message of Jesus and continue his work, even in the face of persecution and opposition. We strategized and planned, determined to honor our Lord's memory and to carry on his mission.

We were also filled with a deep sense of hope, a belief that our Lord's death was not the end, but the beginning of a new and glorious era. Little did we know that soon, our doubts would be dispelled, our fears conquered, and our faith renewed.

But even as we planned and prayed, doubts and fears crept into our hearts. We wondered if we had been mistaken in our belief in Jesus, if his death was truly the end. We struggled to reconcile our faith with the harsh reality of his death and of our own futures.

As the day wore on, we clung to each other, seeking comfort and solace in our shared grief. Our tears mingled together, and our hearts were heavy with sorrow. But even in the depths of our despair, we knew that our Lord was with us. His teachings, his love, and his grace had touched each of us in profound ways, and we were forever changed by his presence in our lives.

We discussed how we would continue Jesus' work without him physically present, and what that would look like. Peter, always the practical one, suggested they focus on healing and teaching, just as Jesus had done. I nodded in agreement, and added that they should also focus on spreading the message of Jesus' love and forgiveness to those who hadn't yet heard it.

James, who had always been the most zealous of the group, spoke up next. "We must also be prepared to suffer," he said. "Jesus warned us that we would face persecution for his sake, and we must be ready for it."

The group nodded solemnly, knowing that their commitment to Jesus might mean facing imprisonment, torture, or even death. But we also knew that our faith was strong enough to withstand any trial.

As they continued to talk, Mary sat quietly in a corner, her grief still palpable. I approached her and put a comforting arm around her shoulder.

"Mary," I said softly, "I know this is hard for you. But you must know that Jesus' death was not in vain. He died to save us all from our sins, and his sacrifice has given us eternal life."

Mary looked up at me with tear-filled eyes. "I know, John," she said. "But it's still so hard to bear. He was my son, my flesh and blood."

I nodded understandingly. "I know, Mary. But you must take comfort in the fact that He is with His Father now, and we will see him again on the Last Day."

Mary smiled weakly, grateful at my words of comfort. She continued "John, Jesus commanded us to be mother and son. I want you to call me mom." I was so touched by her tender words which gave me comfort.

As the night wore on, the group's conversations ebbed and flowed, sometimes focusing on practical matters, sometimes on theological questions, and sometimes on personal memories of Jesus. But through it all, our faith remained strong, and we continued to seek comfort and guidance from God.

In moments of silence, the group would break into hymns of praise and worship, lifting our voices in gratitude for the time they had spent with Jesus. And as dawn approached, they knew that they must face the day ahead with renewed strength and determination.

Again, we were blessed with a great sunny morning peeking through the windows. Mary of Cleopas and Salome, who, with Mary Magdalene, arose earlier to go to the Lord's tomb to anoint his body. Joseph came up the steps with a large jug of juice and bread for us to eat. As we settled down to eat, Mary Magdalene burst into the room with news that the stone was rolled back, the soldiers were not there and that she and the other women were afraid that someone had stolen Jesus' body.

Peter and I jumped up and hugged Mary and told her not to worry, we would find out what happened. Mary Magdalene followed us down the steps in pursuit of us. Peter ran slower than I did and I reached the tomb first. I bent down to look inside and only saw the linens. I waited and Mary arrived next and she said "see, it's just as I told you. He is gone!". Peter then arrived and immediately went inside. He came back out saying that he saw the linen cloths lying there, and the handkerchief that had been over His head, not lying with the linen cloths, but folded together in a place by itself.

Then I went into the tomb. I immediately believed what I recalled Jesus say, that on the third day He would rise again. I had looked for the body of Jesus, but saw only the wrappings that had been around the body were still intact. They were not cut or unwrapped. To me, there was only one answer: Resurrection. Jesus is Risen! As we left the area of the tomb, Mary of Magdala stayed to look for herself.

Simon Peter and I went back to the upper room with great joy in our hearts after I explained to him why I was convinced that Jesus rose from the dead. The group there became cautiously optimistic as I explained why I thought He had risen, then the door flung open and Mary Magdalene stepped in and said that she saw the Risen Lord! As everyone crowded around her, she told of how she asked the gardener if he had taken the body of her Lord. She continued that he simply said "Mary" and that immediately she knew it was Him!

With that, our grief turned to joy and our doubts were be dispelled. But for now, in the upper room, we continued to pray, to mourn, and to seek God's Will for our lives. And even in our darkest moments, we knew that we were not alone, but were surrounded by the love and support of our fellow disciples and apostles while we waited for our own encounters with the Risen Lord!

During that afternoon, Thomas and a few of his friend had ventured out to see if they could find the risen Christ or to try to assess what the reaction of the townspeople may be at the empty tomb. When evening arrived, being the first day of the week, we closed and locked the doors where we assembled, for we all had fear of the Jews, especially since Thomas and his friends had not yet returned. We prayed then began our meal. We heard a noise in what appeared to be from the middle of the room. Jesus appeared and stood in our midst, and said to us, "Peace be with you." Then He showed us His hands and His side. Our fear quickly turned to gladness when we saw the Lord.

Jesus continued, "Peace to you! As the Father has sent Me, I also send you." Then He breathed on us, and said to them, "Receive the Holy Spirit. If you forgive the sins of any, they are forgiven them; if you retain the sins of any, they are retained." With that, He disappeared.

The room was filled with a mix of emotions as the disciples sat together, still in disbelief of what they had just witnessed. Peter quickly arose and checked the lock on the door. It was secure, but immediately, there was a knock from outside. Peter's startled jump nearly hit the ceiling, making many of us laugh. Thomas said "open the door, hurry!" He and his friends said they couldn't find the Risen Jesus and that the town was eerily silent.

"Thomas, it is late and we were worried. Where have you been? You won't believe what just happened," I exclaimed.

Thomas looked around, confused, and asked, "What are you all talking about?"

Peter stepped forward and told him about Jesus' visit, how He had appeared to them and breathed on them, and how they had received the Holy Spirit.

Thomas listened; his brow furrowed in skepticism. "Unless I see the nail marks in His hands and put my finger where the nails were, and put my hand into His side, I will not believe," he said firmly. Then he asked about the Holy Spirit and what this all meant.

The room fell silent as Thomas' words hung in the air. Then Mary spoke up and suggested that we eat first, then after Thomas and his friends had a chance to relax, she would explain the role of the Holy Spirit in Her Life.

After they prayed, read Scripture and broke bread, they feasted on a meal Joseph and his wife prepared for them in celebration of the Resurrection of Jesus.

Then Mary asked them all to grab their candles and meet her at the steps to the attic where she sat. They all gathered around Mary on the steps and gave her their full attention. They could see in her eyes that she had something important to share.

"Peace be with you all," she said, and the apostles responded in kind.

"Brothers and sisters," Mary began, "I want to talk to you about the Holy Spirit. You see, when I was a young girl, the archangel Gabriel came to me and said that the Holy Spirit would come upon me, and that I would bear a child who would save the world from its sins."

The apostles listened intently, knowing the story of Mary's miraculous conception well.

"I want you to understand just how important the Holy Spirit is," Mary continued. "When the Holy Spirit came upon me, I felt a warmth and a lightness in my heart that I had never recognized before. I knew that I was blessed and that I had been chosen for a great purpose."

Mary went on to explain that the Holy Spirit had been with her throughout her life, guiding her, protecting her, and giving her the strength to carry out the will of God. "I never would have been able to endure the pain of watching my Son be tortured, beaten and hung on a cross like a common criminal if it hadn't been for the strength I gained from the Holy Spirit." She told the apostles that they too would need the Holy Spirit in their lives if they were to continue the work that Jesus had started.

"You will also need the Holy Spirit to remind you of all that Jesus taught you," Mary said. "You will need the Holy Spirit to give you the courage to preach the Gospel to all nations, to heal the sick, and to perform miracles in Jesus' name. And you will need the Holy Spirit to keep you safe from harm and to help you carry your own crosses as you share the Good News of my Son, Jesus."

Mary continued, "You know that we are all human... We are so imperfect. We will always be tempted by the evil one as Adam and Eve was in the garden. Jesus knew the hardships and the temptations we would endure, causing us to slip off the path of Righteousness and into sin. Even failing to do what you are called to do is sinful. But through what He did the other day, He has atoned for our sins. All that is needed is to humble ourselves and ask for forgiveness. He told us today that when those who love him, come to you with a contrite heart and profess their sins, thru His suffering, proclaim that their confessed sins are no longer a barrier between them and my Son".

The apostles listened intently, knowing that Mary spoke from a place of deep wisdom and understanding. They knew that the Holy Spirit was the key to their success in carrying out Jesus' mission.

"Thank you for sharing your wisdom with us, Mary," I said. "We will do our best to remember your words and to keep the Holy Spirit with us always."

Mary smiled at me and the other apostles, knowing that they would be successful in their mission as long as they remained faithful to God and filled with the Holy Spirit. She knew that the road ahead would be difficult, but she had faith that her Son's message would continue to spread throughout the world, bringing hope, healing, and salvation to all who believed. She added, "Thomas, I know you were not here when Jesus came and breathed the Holy Spirit upon us. Do not let your heart be troubled, because Jesus will send the full strength of the gifts of the Holy Spirit to us after He ascends into heaven to be with His Father."

Continuing "Jesus will not make you wait too long before He reveals Himself to you as the Risen Christ."

A week later, while they were all gathered together in the upper room, a sudden rush of wind filled the room, and the group felt the presence of the Holy Spirit once again.

Jesus appeared once more, standing before them with a smile on His face. "Peace be with you," He said, turning to Thomas. "Put your finger here; see my hands. Reach out your hand and put it into my side. Stop doubting and believe."

Thomas gasped, staring in disbelief at the wounds in Jesus' hands and side. He fell to his knees, tears streaming down his face, and exclaimed, "My Lord and my God!"

The others in the room looked on in amazement, overwhelmed with joy and awe. They had witnessed the incredible power and love of their Savior once again, and they knew that they would never be the same. Jesus looked around with a smile on His face and said, "so, what is for dinner tonight, I am hungry!".

The Ascension of Jesus

As I looked around the Upper Room, I could sense the solemn silence as the apostles gathered after witnessing the ascension of Jesus into heaven. Our hearts were heavy with mixed emotions, a blend of awe, confusion, and grief. The absence of our beloved Master left a void in our souls, but I knew we were bound together by a shared purpose—to carry forward the message of Christ to the world. It was in this room, permeated with the lingering presence of their departed Lord, that I finally found began to find solace for the first time since He was crucified.

As the sun approached the horizon, I sought the comfort of my brothers, the blessed mother Mary and Mary of Magdala. My heart ached, yet I felt a flicker of hope deep within me when I seem to hear the sound of his footsteps echoed in the near empty room as it felt like He approached Mary, who sat in quiet contemplation, her eyes fixed on a distant memory.

"Mother," I whispered, my voice trembling with both sorrow and anticipation. "How can we go on without Him? His words, His love, His guidance... we were so blessed to have Him."

Mary turned her gaze towards me, her eyes filled with a profound sadness that mirrored my own. "Oh, my dear John," she replied, her voice filled with gentle strength. "Our hearts may be heavy, but we must remember that His spirit lives on within us. He has entrusted us with a sacred mission, to spread His teachings and love to all corners of the earth."

I nodded, my eyes brimming with tears. I could feel the weight of responsibility settle upon my shoulders, the realization of the task ahead. The room continued to fill with the remaining apostles as they returned from their solitary contemplation, their faces etched with grief and wonder.

Peter, once filled with doubt and fear, had become a pillar of leadership. His unwavering resolve and fiery passion inspired the rest of us, urging us to press forward despite the challenges. Peter approached Mary and me, his voice filled with determination and certainty. "We must gather our strength, my friends. The world awaits the message of salvation, and we are the chosen vessels." It was so reassuring to hear the strength in his voice – one which exuded confidence and leadership.

Standing by Peter's side was his brother Andrew and my brother James, both filled with fervor and a burning desire to fulfill their purpose as well. Nonetheless, the air grew heavy with the weight of unspoken fears and doubts. Bartholomew, Thomas, and the others joined the circle, their eyes searching for reassurance amidst the confusion of the day.

I glanced around at my companions, recognizing the unique bond we shared—the experiences, the miracles, and the profound teachings that had woven our lives together. We had become a family, united by their love by and for Christ and our unwavering commitment to His cause.

"Brothers," I said, commanding attention with a steady voice, "we must remember the words of our Lord, 'I am with you always, even unto the end of the age.' He has not abandoned us, but has empowered us with His Spirit. We are not alone."

Thomas, though known for his skepticism, had become a beacon of faith through his unwavering determination to seek truth. His doubts transformed into a fierce desire to understand and experience the risen Christ, and his steadfastness drew others closer to the light of salvation.

I turned to Thomas; my voice continued to be filled with this newfound conviction. "Do not let doubt ever cloud your heart, my brother. We must have faith, for it is through faith that we will find strength. We have witnessed miracles beyond comprehension, and we must trust that He will guide us still."

The room fell into a reflective silence as they pondered my words. Mary, a pillar of faith, radiated a sense of peace amidst the turmoil. She gently placed her hand on my shoulder, her touch infused with motherly love.

"We are bound together in this journey, my dear apostles," Mary said, her voice carrying a serene wisdom. "Together, we will carry the light of Christ to a world in need. Let not your hearts be troubled, for His love will sustain us. And do not forget as He lifted His body above the ground, He told us that He would send another Advocate, the Holy Spirit, to give you powers to be His witness to the ends of the Earth"

As we absorbed Mary's words, a deep sense of purpose began to replace our doubts. Though we still mourned the physical absence of their Lord, we were filled with a renewed determination to spread His message and wondered when the Holy Spirit would completely come upon them.

Time seemed to stand still in the Upper Room as we embraced our shared mission, our hearts kindled with the fire of divine love. We realized that our grief and sorrow were but stepping stones on the path to redemption—a path we were now committed to treading, regardless of the challenges that lay ahead.

In that moment, I knew that they were not alone. The spirit of Jesus Christ, infused within each of us, would guide our every step. And so, with unwavering faith, we embraced the future, ready to become beacons of hope, love, and salvation in a world yearning for the light of Christ thru the Holy Spirit.

Over the next few days, I found solace in Mary's presence. Her unwavering faith and profound understanding of her Son's mission were a source of strength and inspiration for me. We spent hours in prayer and contemplation, seeking guidance and drawing from the wellspring of divine wisdom within them.

One evening, as the sun set and cast its golden glow upon the world, I found myself sharing a quiet moment with Mary in the Upper Room. The flickering light of a solitary candle illuminated their faces, etching lines of wisdom and resolve upon their brows.

"Mom," I began, my voice a mere whisper, "do you ever grow weary? Does the weight of the world ever become too heavy to bear?"

Mary turned her gaze towards me, her eyes brimming with compassion. "My dear John, there are moments when weariness creeps upon my soul, but then I remember the unyielding love of my Son. He bore the weight of the world's sins upon His shoulders, and through His sacrifice, He bestowed upon us the strength to endure."

I nodded; my eyes filled with admiration for the woman before me. "I miss Him, Mother. I miss His voice, His touch. Sometimes, it feels as though a part of me is incomplete without Him."

Mary reached out and gently took my hands in hers, her touch warm and comforting. "You are not alone in your longing, dear John. We all feel the ache in our hearts, the emptiness left by His physical absence. But remember, He is with us still, in every moment, guiding us from within. His love remains alive in our hearts."

She continued, "John, you are such a likable guy. Everyone loves you, but I can tell you that Jesus had a deep agape love for you. He enjoyed watching you grow over these three years physically, emotionally and spiritually. Each one of you guys were chosen to be where you were, as normal guys to build His church upon. You all come from different walks of life – fishermen, tax collectors, politicians, a zealot and businessmen. Each were chosen for their unique mission in His life and the Church He wants you to bring forward. It is so important that you all share His life and why He did what He did with others."

Mary paused, then continued, "The greatest of these reasons is Love. That is the quality He formed in you in your mother's womb, to bring forth from this day, the love He has for all people. He knew that you have that quality to sense love, to take love and multiply it like He did with the loaves and the fishes. To share it, gather the pieces of broken love, mend it and distribute it again." That is why He chose you and held you so close – as the disciple He loved, to shout from the hilltops the love He had for all and died to prove His love for all through the ages."

As I sat in silence, enveloped by the sacred space of the Upper Room, I felt a deep sense of peace wash over me. It was as though he could feel Jesus' presence, a ghostly embrace that whispered words of encouragement and reassurance of what Mary just told me. I will forever consider myself as the one Jesus loved.

Breaking Bread

Peter called us all to gather together to discuss some things Jesus directed us to do at the Passover Meal. It had been a few hours since the Lord's Ascension, and we were still grappling with the weight of His departure. The Upper Room, the place where we had shared the Last Supper with our beloved Master, seemed to be infused with His presence, as if His spirit lingered among us. I took my place, feeling a mix of anticipation and sadness, as we prepared to delve into the instructions He had left us.

As we sat around the room, I couldn't help but glance at the empty seat where Jesus had once sat. His absence was tangible, and it made my heart ache. But we had a task at hand, a responsibility to fulfill His commandments. Peter, who Jesus had given the Keys to the Kingdom, took charge of the proceedings.

"Brothers," Peter began, his voice filled with a mixture of authority and humility, "we have been entrusted with a great mission. Jesus told us to do this in remembrance of Him, and we must ensure that we understand what He meant and how to carry it out."

We nodded in agreement, eager to receive guidance in fulfilling Jesus' wishes. Peter continued, "We must commemorate the breaking of the Bread, just as Jesus did during the Passover Meal. But how should we go about it? What elements should we include?"

My brother James, always thoughtful and introspective, spoke up. "Perhaps we should follow Christ's own example the day of the

Resurrection, on the road to Emmaus. He started by reading the Scriptures, the scrolls of the fathers, explaining the meaning of them, then broke bread. We have been taught by Jesus Himself, and He often referred to the prophecies of old. It would be fitting to include those readings in our commemoration."

Peter nodded, acknowledging the wisdom in James' words. "Yes, the words of the prophets have guided us thus far. We shall incorporate their teachings into our celebration." He turned to me, his gaze earnest. "John, you were closest to Jesus. What do you think? How can we best honor Him?"

I took a moment to gather my thoughts before responding. "Peter, we must also remember the psalms of David. Jesus often recited them, and they resonated deeply within His soul. Let us sing them in praise and thanksgiving, for they capture the essence of His teachings and the depth of His love."

Peter smiled warmly, appreciating the suggestion. "Indeed, the psalms will add a layer of reverence to our remembrance. We shall include them." His eyes then scanned the room, as if searching for further inspiration.

Andrew, ever the observant disciple, spoke up. "The breaking of the bread and the blessing of the wine were the pinnacle of Jesus' ministry. They became His Body and Blood, of His sacrifice for us. We must ensure that these solemn moments are included every time, for they allow us to know He will always remain with us."

Peter nodded in agreement. "Yes, Andrew, you are right. The blessing of the bread and wine and the breaking of the bread are vital. They must remain at the core of our celebration. We shall reenact these sacred rituals, turning them into the true Body, Blood, Soul, and Divinity of Jesus."

As our discussion continued, ideas flowed freely. Thomas proposed incorporating moments of reflection and repentance, as a reminder of our human fallibility and the need for forgiveness. Philip suggested the inclusion of communal prayers, where we would collectively express our gratitude and seek guidance in continuing the Lord's work. Each disciple contributed, weaving their own insights and experiences into the tapestry of our commemoration.

After much deliberation, we had arrived at a plan that captured the essence of Jesus' teachings and His presence among us. It would begin with the reading of the Scriptures, followed by the recitation of the psalms of David, sung in praise and thanksgiving. We would then proceed with the solemn portion of celebrating with the Consecration of the bread and the wine, fully embracing the transformative power of these sacred elements. It was a comprehensive commemoration, carefully crafted to honor Jesus and bring us closer to Him.

With our plan in place, we set about preparing for the first celebration of the breaking of the Bread. We gathered scrolls containing the words of the fathers and meticulously selected passages that spoke of God's promises, redemption, and the return of the Messiah. These verses would serve as a reminder of the prophecies fulfilled in Jesus and reinforce our faith in His divine mission.

Peter, being the natural organizer, arranged the table with care and attention to detail. The bread, representing Jesus' body, was placed at the center, while the cup of wine, symbolizing His blood, sat beside it. We understood the gravity of these elements, recognizing that they held the essence of our salvation.

As the appointed time approached, we assembled in the Upper Room, our hearts filled with a mixture of reverence and anticipation. The air was thick with the lingering presence of our Master, and we could almost feel His gentle touch guiding our every move.

Peter stood in the middle of the table, where Jesus reclined, his voice resolute and strong said "Let us begin in the Name of the Father, the Son, our Lord, Jesus Christ, and the Holy Spirit who remains with us to guide us in all we do and reminds us all that Jesus told us".

Then, Andrew led us in a praise song and read from the scrolls. Then Philip began chanting the psalm of David, then I shared the parable of the fishes and the loaves. Peter continued, "Brothers, let us remember Jesus. Let us partake of the bread and wine, which will be transformed into His very being. And let us do this in memory of Him."

With great solemnity, Peter blessed the bread, raised it high. We all beat of chest and proclaimed "my Lord and my God". Peter lowered and broke the bread, distributing it among us. As we consumed it, we felt an inexplicable connection to Jesus, a communion of spirit that transcended time and space. The bread was transformed into His body, nourishing our souls and reminding us of the sacrifice He had made for our sake.

Next, Peter blessed the wine, raised it high and we immediately knew every drop in that cup was our Lord's Precious Blood. We passed around the cup, its contents deep red color, a poignant reminder of Jesus' shed blood. As the liquid touched our lips, we felt the warmth of His love flow through us, renewing our commitment to His teachings and mission. The wine had become His blood, a living testimony to His eternal covenant with humanity.

Tears streamed down my face as I partook, overwhelmed by the weight of the moment. Jesus' presence was intense, His love enveloping us, binding us together as His disciples. In that sacred space, we understood the true meaning of His words, "Do this in memory of me." It was not a mere ritual; it was an act of profound remembrance, a way to keep His spirit alive within us and share His love with others.

The next day, we went out into the world, carrying the essence of Jesus within us. We carefully distributed His teachings, His compassion, and His transformative power to all who would listen. Our gatherings to commemorate the breaking of the Bread became a source of unity and strength for the early Christian community, a reminder of the bond we shared as followers of the risen Lord.

And so, in the Upper Room, surrounded by the presence of our beloved Master, we discovered the depth and significance of the celebration of the breaking of the Bread. It became a sacred act, a profound testament to Jesus' love and sacrifice. From that day forward, we continued to fulfill His commandments, to gather in His name, and to turn bread and wine into the true Body, Blood, Soul, and Divinity of Jesus, just as He had directed us.

In the days and weeks that followed, our gatherings to commemorate the breaking of the Bread became a central pillar of our faith and community. We carefully nurtured the traditions we had established in the Upper Room, ensuring that each element was carried out with reverence and devotion.

The readings from the Scriptures resonated deeply with us, as we recognized the threads of prophecy and fulfillment woven throughout the sacred texts. The words of the fathers came alive in our hearts, reaffirming our faith in Jesus as the long-awaited Messiah. We found solace in the passages that spoke of His love, His sacrifice, and His ultimate triumph over sin and death.

The psalms of David continued to be a source of inspiration and praise. Their melodies echoed in our souls, carrying our voices upward, bridging the earthly realm with the divine. We sang with all our might, pouring out our gratitude and adoration, allowing the music to lift us to heights of spiritual communion.

But it was in the solemn moments of celebrating the breaking of the bread and receiving the Body and Blood of Jesus. As we gathered around the table, the air thickened with anticipation. Peter's hands trembled ever so slightly as he performed the sacred rituals, mindful of the weight they carried.

We beheld the bread, broken as Jesus had done, and recognized that it was no longer mere sustenance but a gateway to His presence. With each morsel we consumed, we felt the essence of His body infusing our very being, strengthening our faith, and nourishing our souls.

Likewise, the cup of wine, blessed and consecrated, held the indescribable power of His blood. As we partook, a hallowed reverence settled over us, and the knowledge of His sacrifice washed over our hearts. In that moment, we were united with Him, bound by a covenant that transcended time and space.

The commemoration of the breaking of the Bread became more than a remembrance—it was a transformative experience. We were no longer mere disciples; we were carriers of His divine presence. In sharing the bread and wine with one another and with those who sought the truth, we imparted the love, mercy, and grace of Jesus to the world.

Our gatherings became opportunities for fellowship, instruction, and encouragement. We shared stories of Jesus, recounting His teachings, miracles, and the indescribable moments we had shared with Him. The Upper Room, the very place where He had instituted the sacred meal, became a sanctuary of faith and communion.

As we distributed the consecrated bread and wine, we did so with care and intention. It was not a casual act but a sacred responsibility He called for. We approached each person with reverence, knowing that in our hands, we held the embodiment of Christ's sacrifice. We looked into the eyes of those who partook, seeing the hunger for truth, the longing for redemption, and the need for the transformative power that only Jesus could offer.

The memory of Jesus, His life, death, and resurrection, remained vivid in our hearts. His commandment to "do this in memory of me" echoed in our minds with every gathering. And so, we faithfully carried out our duties, carefully preserving the traditions and teachings entrusted to us by our beloved Lord.

Through the breaking of the Bread, we experienced the mystery and wonder of Jesus' presence. We found solace in the rituals that connected us to Him and to one another. In those moments, the Upper Room became a sacred space where the boundaries between heaven and earth blurred, and we glimpsed the eternal love of our Savior.

And so, with hearts aflame and souls renewed, we continued to commemorate the breaking of the Bread in memory of Jesus, fully aware of the profound privilege and responsibility we had been given.

Pentecost

After the powerful outpouring of the Holy Spirit, Mary and John sat together in the upper room, immersed in a deep conversation that revealed the profound impact of that transformative encounter. We knew the Holy Spirit would come upon us, but we didn't know exactly what to expect.

We had a sense of awe and appreciation which filled our hearts. Mom turned toward me with a gentle smile, her eyes radiant with joy. "I am filled with gratitude for what we have witnessed," she said softly. "The Holy Spirit came upon us exactly as Jesus had promised. It was a moment of pure grace and empowerment."

I nodded; my face must have been glowing with a newfound sense of understanding. "Mom, I could feel the presence of the Holy Spirit like a rushing wind, enveloping us in its divine embrace. It was as if a fire had been ignited within our souls, igniting our faith and filling us with a renewed sense of purpose."

The Blessed Mother's eyes sparkled with delight. "Indeed, the Holy Spirit breathed new life into our beings, filling us with its divine fruits. The 12 fruits of the Holy Spirit—charity, joy, peace, patience, kindness, goodness, long-suffering, gentleness, faith, modesty, self-control, and chastity—these perfections are the very essence of holiness. Remember what I said about the fruits of the Holy Spirit which came upon me when I said yes to Gabriel?"

I nodded again, my heart resonating with the truth of her words. "Yes, those fruits will become more evident in our lives as we work to spread the words of Jesus Christ through the whole land. The outpouring of the Holy Spirit transformed us into instruments of love and compassion, radiating the joy of the Gospel to all who encountered us."

Her face lit up, and she spoke with a voice filled with conviction. "The Holy Spirit unifies us and empowers us to live as Christ's witnesses in the world. It brings forth love that is selfless and joyful, peace that surpasses understanding, and the patience to endure trials and hardships. It instills kindness, goodness, and gentleness in our interactions with others. It strengthens our faith and helps us practice modesty, self-control, and chastity."

As we continued our conversation, we marveled at the transformative work of the Holy Spirit in our observations of the others as they shared the Good News of Jesus to the Jewish visitors of Jerusalem from as far away as Libya and Rome, all who heard our brothers speak in our own language, but they understood it in their native language! Hearts overflowed with gratitude by all the brothers for the gifts bestowed upon them, and they vowed to live each day guided by the virtues and fruits of the Holy Spirit, embracing their role as messengers of God's love to the world.

As the Blessed Mother and I reflected on the fruits of the Holy Spirit, they recognized the profound significance of these virtues in their mission to spread the Word of Jesus. Each fruit had a unique role to play in their interactions with others and in the challenges we would face as they proclaimed the Gospel. I asked the Blessed Mother if she would confirm my understanding of the fruits.

Charity, the first fruit, was at the core of our mission. It compels us to love selflessly, to embrace all people as children of God, and to extend acts of kindness and mercy to those in need. Through acts of charity, we demonstrate the love of Christ and invite others to experience His transformative power.

Joy would have to become our constant companion, even in the face of adversity we saw at the crucifixion. The challenges we would encounter will need to be met with unwavering trust and an inner sense of joy that would emanate from our faith in Jesus. I believe a joyful demeanor will attract others, drawing them closer to the Good News and inspiring them to seek a deeper relationship with Christ.

In our encounters with individuals of diverse backgrounds and perspectives, the fruit of peace will guide our interactions. It would help us navigate conflicts, promote understanding, and foster reconciliation. By this fruit of the Holy Spirit presence would become a source of love to those burdened by the worries and strife of the world.

The fruit of patience will sustain us in moments of difficulty and resistance. We will encounter skepticism, opposition, and persecution, but through patience, we will remain steadfast, persevering in our mission. We will understand that God's timing was perfect, and through patience, we will be able to plant seeds of faith that would eventually bear fruit.

Kindness and goodness will shape words and actions, manifesting in acts of compassion and generosity. Through kindness, we'll touch the lives of those we encounter, uplifting spirits and offering glimpses of God's love. Goodness would guide our moral conduct and integrity, ensuring that our lives reflected the teachings of Christ.

The challenges we will face will require resilience and endurance, which would be fortified by the fruit of long-suffering. In times of hardship, we will rely on the strength of the Holy Spirit to carry them through, trusting that our sufferings were united with the redemptive suffering of Christ.

Gentleness will mark our approach, enabling us to reach out to others with humility and understanding. Our words and actions will be characterized by grace, inviting others to embrace the message of Christ with open hearts.

Faith, the foundation of our mission, provides the unwavering conviction and trust in God's promises. It will sustain us during moments of doubt and uncertainty, empowering us to proclaim the Gospel with boldness and conviction.

Modesty will keep our hearts and intentions focused on God's glory rather than our own. We'd humbly acknowledge that our role was to be vessels of God's grace and that the transformative power we will witness is the work of the Holy Spirit.

Self-control and chastity will continue to guide our thoughts, desires, and actions, enabling us to live holy lives in accordance with God's will. Through self-discipline, we will resist temptations and remain steadfast in our commitment to the teachings of Jesus.

Mary was very impressed with how well I understood the mission we were carrying into the future and how the fruits of the Holy Spirit were indispensable tools for spreading the Word of Jesus. We understood that it was through living out these virtues that they would become effective witnesses of Christ's love and draw others into the fold of God's family.

With hearts ignited by the Holy Spirit, we will embark on our mission, allowing these fruits to guide every step. And as we will journey together, we will pray the transformative power of the Holy Spirit will be manifested through our words and deeds, drawing multitudes to the abundant life found in Jesus Christ!

In the Beginning

As I sat with the Blessed Mother Mary in a quiet moment in Jerusalem, I could sense that there was something on her mind. We had been spending more time together in the weeks since Jesus' Ascension and the Descent of the Holy Spirit, sharing memories of his teachings and his life, but there was a sense of urgency in Mary's demeanor that I had not seen before.

Finally, Mary spoke. "John, there is something that has been weighing heavily on my heart. It is about what Jesus told me, and what I know from my personal experience about the Son of the Father before Jesus was conceived."

I leaned in, eager to hear what Mary had to say. "What did Jesus tell you, Mom?"

Her eyes grew misty with emotion. "He told me that He was the Word, the Logos, made flesh. He existed before time began, and He was with God the Father from the beginning. He came into the world to reveal the Father to us, to show us the way to salvation. And He did it all out of love."

I nodded, knowing that these were some of the key themes Jesus talked about. "Yes, Mary, I know. These are some of the things that I have been writing down."

Mary looked at me intently. "But John, you must understand that it is not just enough for you to write these things down. They must be known and believed by people for hundreds of years to come. They

35

must understand that Jesus is not just a teacher or a prophet, but He is the Son of God, the Word made flesh, the Alpha and the Omega."

I could see the passion in Mary's eyes, and felt a sense of responsibility. "I understand, Mary. I will do my best to write the truth about Jesus, so that people may know and believe."

Mary nodded, but she was not finished yet. "But John, it is not just enough to write the truth. You and the others must also live it. You must be an example to others, just as Jesus was. You must love one another, and show hospitality to those who come to you. You must support the missionaries who go out into the world to preach the Word, especially to those who have not yet heard it."

I could see where Mary was going with this. "Are you saying that I should send out missionaries of my own?"

Mary smiled. "Not necessarily, John. But it is clear that the eleven of you will need help. You will each need to gather a few to travel with when you travel out on your mission trips. And when others are out on their missions, you can support those who are already out there."

I nodded, taking in Mary's words. "I will remember this, Mom. Thank you for your guidance and your wisdom."

Mary smiled at him. "You are welcome, John. Just remember, Jesus is the Word made flesh, and he came to reveal God to us. It is up to us to spread that message, to live it out, and to support those who are doing the same."

I took a deep breath, allowing the weight of Mary's words to settle in my heart. I had never thought of it that way before. I had always known that Jesus was special, but to think that He existed before the world was even created? It was mind-boggling to think that Jesus, although Divine, came to this dreadful place to save us from our own sins and He knew my in my mother's womb, planting in my growing mind how to love as He loves.

"But how do we share this with others?" I asked, turning to Mary. "How do we make people understand the divine nature of Christ and the importance of His role in our salvation?"

Mary smiled softly; her eyes full of wisdom. "We tell them what we know," she said. "We share our personal experiences with Jesus. We tell them about the miracles we witnessed, the love He showed us, and the way He changed our lives. And we trust that the Holy Spirit will work in their hearts to reveal the truth to them."

I nodded, feeling a sense of peace wash over me. I had always known that the Holy Spirit was powerful, but to think that it could work in the hearts of others to reveal the truth of Christ's divine nature was humbling.

As we sat there in silence, I felt a renewed sense of purpose in my writing. I knew that I had a great responsibility, but I also knew I was not alone. With Mary's guidance and support, and with the power of the Holy Spirit, I would continue to spread the message of Jesus to all who would hear it, in person and in the stories Mary encouraged us to write about.

"I will continue to share what I know," I said, looking at Mary with determination. "I will write it down so that it can be shared for generations to come. And I will pray that the Holy Spirit works in the hearts of those who hear the message."

Mary placed a hand on my shoulder, her touch gentle and reassuring. "I know you will, my son," she said. "And I will be here to support you every step of the way. We are both witnesses to the truth, and it is our responsibility to share it with others."

For a few moments, Mary and I sat in silence, taking in the beauty of the garden around us. The sun was starting to set, casting a warm glow over everything. I couldn't help but feel grateful for this moment of quiet reflection with Mary.

As we stood up to leave, Mary turned to me with a final word of encouragement. "Remember, my son," she said, "it is not just about sharing the truth of Christ's Divinity, but also about living out that truth in our daily lives. Let us be examples of His love and grace to everyone we meet."

I nodded, with a clear sense of purpose. I knew that this conversation with Mary would stay with me for the rest of my life, guiding me as I shared the truth of Christ's existence from the beginning of time. I will live out that truth in my own life, assured that Jesus, His Father and the Holy Spirit always were and always will be, forever and ever!

And as I walked away from the garden with Mary by his side, I knew that I would not be alone. I had the support and guidance of the Blessed Mother, who had been entrusted with so much knowledge and understanding of the Son of God. Together, we would continue to share the truth of Christ's Divinity, trusting in the Holy Spirit to work in the hearts of all who hear the message.

Signs and Miracles

One evening in the quiet moments of the evening in Jerusalem after we broke bread together, Mary's thoughts turned to her son's miracles and signs, and the reason why he performed them. I could sense the emotion in her voice as she spoke, and he leaned in to listen more closely.

"John, my son," Mary began, "do you remember the turning of water into wine at the wedding in Cana?"

"Yes, mom," I replied, "I remember it well. It was one of the first miracles Jesus performed."

"Indeed it was," Mary said, a hint of a smile on her lips. "But do you understand the significance of it?"

I furrowed my brow, unsure of what she meant. "I'm not sure, mom. What do you mean?"

"John, my dear, it was more than just a simple act of turning water into wine. It was a sign of who He was, and what He came to do," Mary said, her voice gaining strength. "He was revealing His divine nature, His power to transform the ordinary into the extraordinary, to bring joy and celebration where there was none."

I sat back, my mind whirling with this new insight. I had always known that Jesus' miracles were more than mere acts of kindness or compassion. But to hear Mary speak of them in this way, as signs of His true identity, opened up a whole new realm of understanding.

"But what of the healing of the blind man?" I asked, eager to learn more. "What was the significance of that?"

Mary's eyes softened as she remembered that day. "John, my son, that was a sign of his compassion and his power over sickness and suffering. But it was also a sign of something deeper, something that he shared with me."

"What was it, mother?" I asked, hanging on her every word.

"John, he told me that he was the light of the world, that he came to bring sight to the blind, both physically and spiritually," Mary said, her voice filled with emotion. "He was revealing to me his divine mission, and his love for all of humanity."

I sat in silence, letting Mary's words wash over me. I knew that these miracles and signs were not just random acts of kindness, but were powerful statements of who Jesus was and what he came to do.

"But what of the raising of Lazarus from the dead, mother?" I asked, my curiosity piqued. "Surely that was the greatest miracle of all."

Mary's face grew solemn as she recalled that day. "Yes, my son, it was. But it was also a sign of his power over death and his promise of eternal life."

I leaned forward, my eyes locked onto Mary's. "And what did Jesus tell you about it, mother? What did he reveal to you?"

Mary's voice dropped to a whisper as she spoke. "John, my son, he told me that He was the resurrection and the life, that whoever believed in Him would never die but have eternal life."

I sat back in awe, his mind reeling with this new understanding. I knew that these miracles and signs were not just demonstrations of Jesus' power, but were deeply meaningful expressions of His love and divine mission.

As we sat together in the quiet of the evening, Mary and I shared a moment of deep understanding and reverence for the miracles and signs that Jesus had performed. And I knew that these were truths that

I would carry with him for the rest of my life, a testament to the power and love of my Savior and friend.

Mary sighed deeply; her eyes still fixed on the horizon. "But it wasn't just about proving who he was, John. He performed these miracles out of love and compassion for the people. He saw their suffering and their pain, and he couldn't just stand idly by and watch. He had to do something."

I nodded, listening intently. "And what about the people who didn't believe, who rejected him despite witnessing these miracles?"

Mary turned to face me; her expression pained. "It broke his heart, John. He loved them so much, but they refused to see the truth. He knew that some would reject him, but it still hurt him deeply."

I nodded in understanding, his own heart heavy with the weight of Jesus' suffering. "And what about the future, Mom? What will happen to the knowledge of these miracles and signs?"

Mary's gaze grew intense. "That is why it is so important for us to tell His story, John. To share with others what we have witnessed and what we know to be true. We must not let his miracles be forgotten or misunderstood. They are a testament to His divine nature and His love for us."

I nodded in agreement; my resolve strengthened. "I will do everything in my power to ensure that his message is heard and that his miracles are remembered. Thank you, Mom, for sharing your insights with me."

Mary smiled softly, placing a gentle hand on my shoulder. "You have always been a faithful disciple, John. I have no doubt that you will continue to spread his message with love and compassion, just as He did."

Capturing His Teachings

Mary urged me to document all His teachings for future generations. She knew that they would be a source of comfort and guidance for those who would come after us, and she did not want them to be lost or forgotten. She spoke passionately of her own experience of hearing Jesus speak these words, and how they had shaped her faith and her understanding of who He was.

I listened to her with deep respect and admiration, knowing that she had been a faithful disciple and witness of Jesus from the very beginning. Her words inspired me to reflect on the importance of preserving the teachings and discourses of Jesus, not only for the benefit of those who would come after us, but also for our own continued growth in faith and understanding.

She spoke with such passion and conviction, as if the words of her beloved son were still ringing in her ears. I knew that these teachings were unlike anything else that my brothers were writing about and I needed to capture them.

We prayed for guidance and wisdom, and we asked the Holy Spirit to help us to remember all that Jesus had said. And in the end, I was moved to write down these words, so that others might come to know and believe in Jesus Christ, the Son of God, and have eternal life in Him.

Between Mary and the wisdom of the Holy Spirit, I had a heart brimming with the depths of our encounters with Jesus! It is such a pleasure to embark on a journey of memories through the profound teachings that unfolded while I was in the presence of the Word made flesh. These words cannot fully capture the majesty and weightiness of the moments shared with my beloved Teacher. But may they be testament to the truths we beheld and the eternal life we were called to proclaim.

Although I don't feel worthy to recount and document the very essence of Christ's identity as the Word of God, I certainly will try! Through Him, all things were made, and in His earthly dwelling, we experienced the fullness of grace and truth. Our hearts burned as we heard Him speak; His words resonating with divine authority and wisdom. The profound teachings that unfolded from His lips unveiled mysteries beyond human comprehension, unveiling the nature of God's love and the path to eternal life.

I witnessed the transformative power of Jesus' miracles and the profound lessons they imparted. From turning water into wine at the wedding in Cana to healing the sick and raising the dead, His works affirmed His divine authority and revealed glimpses of the kingdom of God breaking into our broken world. Through these wondrous acts, He taught us to have faith, to trust in His power, and to live with a conviction that transcended the boundaries of earthly limitations.

I bear witness to the radical nature of the message of Jesus, challenging the prevailing religious norms of our time. Through parables, analogies, and powerful metaphors, Jesus illuminated profound truths about the Kingdom of God, inviting us to embrace a spiritual rebirth and an intimate union with the Father. His teachings spoke directly to the depths of our souls, awakening within us a hunger for righteousness and a desire to abide in Him, the true vine that sustains our lives.

I asked Mary to recount some of His discourses in detail, so that I could make sure I got it correctly documented. Mary agreed, her voice growing stronger with each passing moment. She spoke of Jesus' profound teachings on love, forgiveness, and compassion, and of his promise to send the Holy Spirit to guide and comfort his followers.

Hours passed and the sun began to set on Jerusalem, Mary and I were mentally exhausted and we sat in silence, lost in thought. I knew that I had been given a great responsibility, but I also knew that I had been given a great gift. I felt as if Jesus himself had entrusted me with a sacred task, and I would honor that trust with every fiber of his being.

In the days that followed, I began to write. I poured himself into this work, transcribing my notes of Mary's recollections of Jesus' teachings and discourses with great care and attention to detail. I knew that this was not just an exercise in recording history, but a sacred task that had been entrusted to me by Jesus himself.

Faith and Belief

In the seven years since our Lord ascended into heaven, we have been very busy spreading the Word of Jesus' Love and Forgiveness in the areas around Jerusalem and the countryside of Judea as well as trying to figure out how to effectively identify ourselves as followers of Jesus Christ. Most of the Jewish leaders remained angry at the teachings of Jesus and continued to feel threatened of us sharing the Good News to all.

They still have many in the Roman Army sympathetic to their plight, so many who followed the Way of Jesus had to hide from both the Jews and the Romans. They would round up members of the Way and bring them to jail. Many of them didn't ever come back to their wives and children. We used money donated to the cause of the Way to help widows and orphans as best as we could, but as our numbers increased, so did those arrested and carried away. Most were willing to endure the sufferings to add to the sufferings of Jesus, their new Master. Many were willing to follow Him to the cross, as they knew from their teachings of Jesus, Eternal Life is well worth the sufferings in this life.

We received word from Ananias of Damascus that Saul of Tarsus, a devout Jew as well as a Roman citizen was staying at the home of Judas on Straight Street. Ananias had been visited by the Lord Himself and told to go to Judas' house and lay hands on Saul, for in his zeal for persecuting His followers, he was persecuting Him. Witnesses claim Saul was knocked off his horse and when he got up from the ground was blinded. Others traveling with Saul watched as the bright light flashed in their own eyes, but only Saul was blinded. He claimed that he talked to Jesus, who told him to stop persecuting Him. As the others led Saul to Damascus, he repented his wrong doing in capturing and torturing the followers of Jesus and recommended the others to repent as well.

Ananias knew Straight Street well, as it was the longest street in the city. Damascus was laid out as a rectangle and Straight Street split the rectangle in half, making Straight Street very accessible from both sides. Ananias wrote in his message to us that he was extremely worried that it was some type of trap. Everyone knew about Saul. He was ruthless to all of Jesus' followers. Yet he was asked in the vision of Jesus to do so. Ananias was wrote that he prayed every step of the way that if he was captured, he would not give up his friends names or their locations where they broke bread together. Once at Judas' house, he was invited in immediately and brought to Saul. Ananias' prayers over Saul commanded the scales covering Saul's eyes to fall, and one by one they dropped onto the floor. Saul and Judas immediately asked to be baptized and receive the Holy Spirit.

At nearly the same time, Herod Agrippa was appointed King of Judea and Samaria. We worried about how this would impact our mission of spreading the Word, especially because Philip has been in Samaria for a few weeks and was met with open minds and hearts. We heard that with loud shrieks, impure spirits came out of many, and many who were paralyzed or lame were healed. So there was great joy in that city.

Mary had shared with me a message Jesus had told her about how we always hear about the sad people, for they typically tell everyone how sad they are. Happy people might show a smile but sometimes it takes just a small act of kindness to watch their joy to bloom like a flower in the sun. We must all remember these words of Jesus.

But like all things, Philip sent to us a messenger to tell us an Angel of the Lord came upon him and directed Philip to go to Jerusalem then to Gaza. Peter asked me to prepare to join him in a trip to Samaria to continue the momentum that Philip had started. Mother Mary told me to go, that She would be safe with the others in Jerusalem until my return. Peter and I began to pack for the journey so we could leave the morning after Philip returned to Jerusalem.

Later, I saw Mary in the garden. She shared with me again, her concern about the need for people to believe in Jesus as the Son of God. "John, my son," she began, "you know better than most how much Jesus emphasized the importance of belief and faith in Him. 'Believe in me,' He said, 'and you will have eternal life.' This was a central theme throughout His ministry, and yet I fear that many have forgotten its significance." Make sure you tell the Samaritans this in your journeys as well.

I nodded in agreement. I too had witnessed the transformative power of belief in Jesus, and I understood the urgency of Mary's message. "Tell me more, Mother," I urged.

Mary took a deep breath and continued. "From the very beginning, Jesus knew that belief in Him and His Father was the key to salvation. He told Nicodemus that 'whoever believes in Him will not perish but have eternal life.' And when Martha questioned Him about the resurrection, He declared, 'I am the resurrection and the life. The one who believes in me will live, even though they die.'"

Mary smiled and said, "There will always be wonderous events in this world, but the joy of the Resurrection will always be the greatest!". Mary continued, "John, think about it. His mission was to share the good news to all about the wonders of the eternal life after this life and to die a sacrificial death for the remission of sins of those who repent and accept His forgiveness. But He brought it all full circle in the Resurrection. Without it, there would be doubt in the entire message."

John listened intently as Mary recounted various instances when Jesus emphasized the importance of belief and trust in Him, including the story of the healing of the paralyzed man in Capernaum and the feeding of the five thousand.

"Belief was the foundation of Jesus' ministry," Mary explained. "He performed many miracles to show people that He was indeed the Son of God, and that belief in Him was the way to eternal life. But even then, some refused to believe."

I sighed at the memory of those who had rejected Jesus despite witnessing His miracles. "It's hard to understand why some people refuse to believe," I said.

Mary nodded in agreement. "Yes, it is," she replied. "But Jesus knew that not everyone would believe. He told the Jews, 'you do not believe because you are not my sheep.' But to those who did believe, He promised that they would never perish."

As we sat in silence for a moment, I reflected on the incredible power of faith. I thought of the many people I had encountered who had been transformed by their faith in Jesus, and I understood why Mary was so concerned about the importance of belief and faith.

"But Mother, how can we ensure that people continue to believe?" I asked.

Mary smiled at my question. "By sharing the message of Jesus with others," she said. "By telling them about His teachings and His miracles, and by reminding them of the importance of faith. We must never forget to tell them that Jesus is the way, the truth, and the life, and that faith in Him is the key to salvation."

I bowed in agreement. I understood the urgency of Mary's message, and I was grateful for her guidance and wisdom. We continued to speak of the many ways in which faith in Him had transformed their own lives, and we prayed that others would come to know the transformative power of faith in the Son of God and how those who believed in Him would have eternal life.

Mary shared a specific moment when Jesus spoke of this in the synagogue in Capernaum, after he had fed the 5,000 with only five loaves and two fish. The people were amazed by the miracle and came to Jesus, asking him what they needed to do to do the works of God. Jesus responded, "This is the work of God, that you believe in Him whom He has sent."

Mary emphasized that Jesus' message was not just about performing good deeds or following religious laws, but about placing one's trust in him as the Messiah and the Son of God. She recalled how Jesus once asked his disciples, "Who do you say that I am?" and how Peter had replied, "You are the Christ, the Son of the living God."

Mary spoke of how this confession of faith was the foundation of the Church and how Jesus promised that the gates of hell would not prevail against it. She reminded me of the "Great Commission", as she called it, that Jesus gave to his disciples before his ascension, to go and make disciples of all nations, baptizing them in the name of the Father and of the Son and of the Holy Spirit, and teaching them to obey everything that he had commanded them.

As I listened to Mary's words, I felt a renewed sense of purpose and commitment to the mission that Jesus had given us and more importantly the trip to Samaria that Peter and I would embark upon soon. I realized that belief and faith in Jesus was not just a matter of personal salvation, but a call to share the good news with others and to make disciples of all nations.

Once again, I thanked Mary for sharing these insights with me and promised to write this all down and continue to preach the message of belief and faith in Jesus as the Son of God to all who would hear it. I knew that the road ahead would be difficult and filled with challenges, but I also knew that with God's grace and the guidance of Mary's wisdom, we could overcome anything that lay before us.

Philip arrived in Jerusalem and after he rested and cleaned up, we all gathered and broke bread in Thanksgiving. Philip left for Gaza as

Peter and I left for Samaria. We were met by an enthusiastic crowd in Samaria! Philip did a great job evangelizing and teaching the Good Word. Peter and I took turns preaching about how the Word taught to us by Jesus were something to remember as much as we remember the words on the scrolls.

We reinforced what Phillip had told them to love God the best you can, that He loves all of us, regardless of where we grew up and that He would never abandon us. The Samaritan disciples cried out that the Holy Spirit also will never leave us. We knew that Philip had done well and we broke bread with them and returned to Jerusalem.

More Sadness, Then Joy

Over the next couple years we all were centralized in Jerusalem, taking trips of a few weeks to a few months to neighboring towns and villages. This also let us get a chance to really get to know Saul on a personal level. Since his conversion, there hasn't been the widespread prosecution of Jesus' followers. We also decided to follow the lead that Jesus made in giving new names to some of us after a life changing event.

We even teased Saul and initially called him "basket boy", which he hated and told us it was the only way he would be able to sneak out of Damascus. We all have been through those life-threatening moments, but ironically, many were due to Saul's previous life. So, Paul was the name everyone agreed upon, and he liked it also.

The church was growing and all were filled with the Holy Spirit, just as it came upon us. Even the Gentiles joined us and Peter invited them to the church without converted to the Jewish Faith first! But like all good things, Herod and the Jewish leaders became increasingly jealous and angry. They harassed members of the church and took my brother James into custody. The next day, I was told that Herod murdered James! He was beheaded, just like John, the Baptist. The Jewish leaders were very pleased that James was made an example of things to come. I wept bitterly at this news.

Then I heard that the following day, the feast of Unleavened Bread, they tracked down Peter. I didn't know what would become of Peter, the rest of us Apostles and the church. I needed answers and the compassion only a mother could give.

John and Mary sat in silence for a few moments, the weight of their conversation about the life and ministry of Jesus lingering heavily between them. Finally, I spoke up, my voice soft but steady.

"Mother, I have been thinking a great deal about the events that led up to Jesus' crucifixion and resurrection. It is still hard to believe that he willingly endured such suffering and death for us. And now James is gone and Peter is in Jail."

Mary's face was etched with pain as she remembered those terrible days and also relating them to the situation now. "It was a difficult time, my son. But Jesus always knew what he had to do. He told us many times that he would have to suffer and die in order to save us." Then she continued, "James knew this well and yet he continued to put himself in harms way. Peter is doing the same and may have the same fate."

John nodded. "Yes, I remember Jesus saying that. But it is still hard for me to fully comprehend what he went through. The beatings, the mockery, the pain of the cross..."

Mary placed a hand on John's arm. "My dear son, it was more than just physical suffering that Jesus endured. He carried the weight of the world's sin on his shoulders. He took upon himself the punishment that we all deserved. And he did it out of love for us."

John's eyes misted over as he thought about the enormity of what Jesus had done. "He truly was the Son of God, wasn't he, Mother? The way he faced his death with such courage and love...no one else could have done that."

Mary smiled through her tears. "Yes, my son, Jesus was the Son of God. And his sacrifice was not just for us, but for the whole world. He showed us what it truly means to love and to lay down our lives for others. We must follow his example and be willing to carry our own crosses, no matter how heavy they may be. That is what gave James the strength to give up his life for the Way."

John nodded solemnly. "I understand, Mother. And I will do my best to live up to Jesus' example and if necessary, I will give up my life like my brother James."

Mary leaned in closer to John. "Remember, my son, that Jesus' story did not end with his death on the cross. He rose from the dead on the third day, just as he had promised. And that is the greatest proof of his divinity and his love for us as well as giving us hope for our own eternal life."

John smiled, feeling a glimmer of hope amidst the darkness of their discussion. "Yes, you're right, Mother. The resurrection is our ultimate source of hope and faith. Do you think James also will rise?"

Mary exclaimed, "Yes, you will see him in the resurrection on the last day."

They sat in quiet reflection for a few moments longer, the reality of Jesus' sacrifice and resurrection settling deep within their hearts. Finally, John stood up, a sense of purpose and determination filling him.

"I will do my best to share this message of hope and love with others, Mom. To tell them about Jesus and his sacrifice, and to show them what it means to truly believe in him, even to the point of sacrificing my life."

Mary stood up as well, her eyes shining with pride and love. "I know you will, my dear son. And I will always be here to support and guide you in your mission."

With that, they embraced, the love and bond between them stronger than ever before. And as they parted ways, they both knew that the legacy of Jesus' life and ministry would continue on, through the power of belief and faith in him as the Son of God.

I felt a renewed sense of purpose and passion for his work, knowing that it was not just about recording historical events, but about preserving the message of hope, love, and faith that Jesus had brought to the world.

With Mary's guidance and the strength of my own convictions, I knew that he would continue to spread the good news of Jesus Christ to the ends of the earth, just as Jesus had commanded him to do.

Pack your bags

I said to Mary, "Mom, I know that you want to stay here in Jerusalem and continue to minister to the sick and elderly. But we are still in a famine and many are struggling to figure out how to feed their families. Many of them are stealing and some are actually killing just for fragments of a loaf of bread for their children".

Mary replied, "I would rather starve and give the last measures of flour I have to a younger mom with babies to feed that to let them go unnourished".

"I know mom. I was thinking that Peter will be leaving Tarsus in a few days for Antioch. He would love to see you! We could gather together in Ephesus. Ephesus right now, is a much safer city for you and it is right on the sea. We are fishermen and can catch whatever we need to eat. There are many Greeks who have yet to hear the Good News. I think the Holy Spirit is guiding us there. "

My beloved son John, my heart overflows with the love of our Lord Jesus Christ for you and for all those who will come to believe through your testimony. I know that you have been anointed by the Holy Spirit to proclaim the truth about Jesus Christ, and that you have been called to shepherd and guide God's people through your writings.

As I look upon you, I see the passion and fire in your eyes, and I know that you are eager to share with the world all that you have learned and experienced about our Lord Jesus Christ. But let me remind you, my dear son, that your words must be grounded in truth, in love, and in the power of the Holy Spirit.

You have walked with Jesus, talked with Him, and witnessed His life, death, and resurrection. You have seen the power of the Holy Spirit at work in your life and in the lives of others. You have experienced the joy of fellowship with the Father and the Son. These experiences and encounters have shaped your understanding of who Jesus is and what it means to follow Him.

Now, my dear son, it is time to share what you have learned with others. It is time to put pen to paper and write down what you have seen and heard. Write with boldness and conviction, knowing that the truth you proclaim will set people free from the bondage of sin and death.

Write about the love of God that was demonstrated in the life, death, and resurrection of Jesus Christ. Write about the power of the Holy Spirit to transform lives and renew minds. Write about the assurance and confidence that comes from knowing Jesus as Lord and Savior. Write about the importance of love, obedience, and fellowship in the life of the believer.

But also, my son, be aware of the false teachings and the deceivers who seek to lead people astray. Warn the people of the dangers of false teachings and encourage them to hold fast to the truth of the gospel. Let them know that they are not alone, but that they are part of a community of believers who love and support one another.

My dear John, I know that you have been chosen for such a time as this. I know that you will write with passion, with conviction, and with the guidance of the Holy Spirit. I pray that your words will bring life, hope, and salvation to those who read them. And I pray that God will bless you and keep you, now and forevermore.

Mary continued, "John, you can do that here in Jerusalem or in Ephesus or anywhere in the world. I will begin to pack in the morning for our trip to Ephesus." I smiled and told her how much I loved her!

Mission of the City by the Sea

After a long trip, we finally arrived at Ephesus. This will be home for quite a while, at least until the famine passes. As Mary and I approached the city, we heard of a man who was preaching of Jesus, but some of the doctrine we heard of from others, we knew it wasn't one of ours. This false doctrine, mixed with profession of Jesus while living a life of sin will have to be addressed very quickly!

After getting settled into our new home, Mary and I ventured out toward the docks in search for something to eat. There was a small group on the shore with a nice fire being blown by the winds of the sea. They asked if we'd like to join them. They had just finished eating and had some fish and bread left which they offered us. One of the men had a flute and was playing songs that the others knew. Unfortunately, I knew enough conversational Greek language, but not the informal and songs. They were very catchy tunes, but we didn't know the words or what they meant. We enjoyed the company they provided.

They asked us many questions about how it was like to live in Jerusalem. We mentioned that every place, big or small has good points and bad points. I said the diversity in Jerusalem was interesting, although unless you are in lock step with the Jewish Leaders, they use the Roman army and the temple guard to suppress anything spoken against them or their corrupt distortions of the Jewish Faith.

One of the men said that he had recently returned from a short trip to Nazareth and stopped in Tarsus for several days and listened to a man talk about a man who they believed was the Messiah. He said that the Jewish leaders had him crucified but He rose from the dead after 3 days. The preacher said that this man was from Nazareth! I only went to Nazareth to get some wool for my textile business, so I didn't get into many discussions with the people there.

Mary spoke up and said, "That was my son, Jesus of Nazareth! He is no longer here; He went to His Father in Heaven. His mission was to show all the light of His Father. This world if full of darkness and now, we have seen a great light, and that light was Jesus. John, tell them about Jesus".

I said, "Oh, how I long for you to hear the depth and breadth of the incredible experience we had with Jesus Christ, the Son of God, the Word made flesh. I walked with Him, talked with Him, and witnessed firsthand the love and compassion He had for His fellow man. I saw Him heal the sick, feed the hungry, and raise the dead. I heard Him speak of the kingdom of God, of righteousness and justice, and of the grace and mercy that flow from the heart of the Father. The problem is we just got here from a long trip and we are both very tired. Can we meet tomorrow?"

They all agreed, that it was getting late. One said "Let's meet at the Mosaic at midafternoon for tea".

Mary and I ventured out the next day to meet our new friends at the Mosaic. It had been very hot all day, so we were glad to meet them past the mid-day sun. We heard one of our new friends call out "John, Mary, we are over here". Thanks be to God they had a location in the shade overlooking the Mosaic. They had a pot filled with tea. I was lukewarm, which was fine with me. It quenched my thirst!

In the light of the sun, we could more clearly associate names with faces. Luciana was married to Martin, Dionysius to Adriana and their friend who had traveled to Nazareth, Antonius. They all grew up in Ephesus but seemed to be pretty free-thinking people. They were all closer to my age, but a little older than me.

Mary told me earlier in the day that when we met up with them, it is not enough to simply recount the events of our time with Jesus. We must also explain their significance. We must help others understand what it means to have a relationship with the Son of God, to be a follower of Jesus Christ. We must make clear that the forgiveness He brought us was not just for us alone, but for all who would believe. We must share the hope that He gave us, the hope of eternal life that is available to all who trust in Him.

She said, "And we must not stop there, my dear John. We must also address the false teachings that threaten to lead people astray. We must warn against those who would try to deceive God's children and lead them down a path of destruction. We must be bold in our proclamation of the truth, unafraid to speak out against those who would seek to undermine the message of Jesus Christ."

So that is what I did. I told them about being a fisherman and mending our nets. I told them how intrigued I was when He said "come with me and I will make you fishers of men". I continued, "I had no clue what He was talking about, but when He said that and kept walking without looking back, my brother James and I dropped our nets and ran after Him." Then I worked my way through what Mary suggested, looking over at her, seeking some kind of assurances that I was on track. I love Jesus so much, sometimes I get carried away.

The more I spoke of Jesus, the more they would lean in to hear every word. They were really very interested in all the details. I tried my best to reinforce that love is the very heart of the Jesus' message. I said, "It was love that brought Jesus to the earth, love that inspired His sacrifice, and love that binds us all together as brothers and sisters in Christ. We must let our words be a reflection of that love, pointing people towards the eternal love and grace of our Lord and Savior." Luckily, Antonius interrupted a few times saying that my message was almost word for word the testimony that the guy in Tarsus had said.

Antonius said, "(Peter) had said that we can not live two lives, one when with one set of friends, and the other with other friends".

I said, "Yes, Antonius, you are absolutely correct! We not only deceive others, but we lie to ourselves. We can not seek forgiveness of our sins when we live 2 lives like that".

Luciana spoke up, "How do we ask to forgive our sins if Jesus is with His Father in Heaven?"

"Well, Luciana, deep down inside, when we sin, we know that we did something offensive. Sometimes, we try to cover it up with a lie and more deception." "The friend we lied to, may forget, but if it caused them a lot of pain, they will remember it", I said. Then I said, "If you ask Jesus sincerely for forgiveness, He forgives you!" I continued, "One of the last things he told those of us Apostles before He ascended into Heaven, was that all sins we forgive, are forgiven, but those we retain are retained".

All five of them asked to be baptized in Jesus' name, sought forgiveness for their sins and begged for the Holy Spirit! I was so happy! Mary suggested that we ask them over to our house to break bread, the way that Jesus taught us, so we did. From that moment, they because active disciples for Jesus and helped me make serious progress in evangelizing and sharing the Word of Jesus Christ in Ephesus.

Gathering of Friends

This afternoon Peter should arrive from Antioch. It will be so good to see him! I am anxious to show him around Ephesus and introduce him to our great friends Dionysius and Adriana, Luciana and Martin as well as Antonius. It's been a few months since Antonius stood in the crowd in Tarsus to hear him speak, but I know Antonius is excited to see Peter again. They want to introduce us to a friend of theirs, Apollo. He is another Greek who apparently knows Paul!

Mary and I had a wonderful breakfast with fresh eggs, oranges and figs. She asked me for an update on my writings. She seemed very disappointed that I had not made much progress. I told her that I have been preaching and teaching to preach every opportunity I had. But I get her point. Jesus, Stephen and my own brother are examples of lives cut short.

Mary urged, "continue to write down every detail of these miraculous events. Do not leave anything out, no matter how small or insignificant it may seem. Describe the way Jesus looked, the tone of His voice, and the expressions on His face. Recall the conversations you had with Him, the questions you asked, and the answers He gave. Let your words paint a vivid picture of the Savior that the world may know Him as we did."

She continued, "I implore you to write down these words. Let your pen be guided by the Holy Spirit, that what you write may be a powerful witness to the truth of Jesus Christ. Let your message be one of hope, of love, and of truth, that all who read it may be drawn closer to the heart of God. They must know the extend of the love that the Father had for all on Earth that He sent His only Son, knowing that the evil one would spread jealousy which would lead to His sacrificial death."

She continued, "As you write, my dear son, remember that you are not alone in this task. The Holy Spirit is with you, guiding you, inspiring you, and empowering you to do the work that God has called you to do. And you have the support of your fellow disciples, who are also laboring for the sake of the good news. Together, we can make a difference in the world, sharing the teachings of Jesus Christ with all who will listen."

"But even as we write the good news, we must also live out the message that we proclaim." Mary went on to say, "We must be the hands and feet of Jesus in a broken and hurting world. We must love our neighbors as ourselves, showing compassion to those who are suffering, and reaching out to those who are lost. We must be willing to lay down our lives for the sake of the Good News, just as Jesus did for us."

And I interjected, "we must remain steadfast in our faith, even when the world around us seems to be falling apart. We must cling to the hope that we have in Christ, knowing that He has overcome the world and that one day, He will return to set all things right. We must encourage one another, building each other up in the faith, and praying for one another that we may be strengthened for the journey ahead."

Mary exclaimed "My dear John; remember that the message of the Good News is not reserved for a select few. It is for all people, regardless of their race, ethnicity, social status, or background. Jesus came to save the whole world, and our message must reflect that reality. We must be willing to cross cultural barriers, to reach out to those who are different from us, and to share the love of Christ with all who will receive it. Ephesus appears to be a great place to share the Good News of Jesus!"

"And so, my dear John, I conclude with these words. May they inspire you, challenge you, and encourage you as you seek to fulfill the calling that God has placed on your life. May your words be a powerful witness to the truth of Jesus Christ, and may your life be a shining example of His love and grace. May we all, as His disciples, follow in His footsteps, sharing the good news of salvation with all who will listen, and bringing hope and healing to a world in need."

"Mother Mary, look, there is Peter!" I said. "Peter, we are over here! Come and sit down. May the Peace of Jesus Christ be with you!" Then he responded, "And with your spirit, my brother! Mother Mary, you look beautiful, as always."

Mary said, "Peter, be gentle with John. I just lectured him about his duty to document the details of his life with Jesus". Peter responded that he was exhausted from his walk anyway and just wanted a drink of water and a 2-hour nap.

I said, "Well, we can set you up with both. Let's show you where we live. I hope you will be rested enough to join us for the Breaking of the Bread at our new Gathering Place. Our Greek friends call our gatherings to Break Bread an 'ekklēsia'. You will like them." Peter said "I look forward to both!"

As the golden rays of the late afternoon sun bathed the streets of Ephesus in a warm glow, I found myself overjoyed walking alongside my dear friend Peter again. Of course, the absence of James tugged at my heart. The day had been filled with anticipation, for we were about to gather with our fellow brothers and sisters in Christ at the Gathering Place, for the sacred breaking of the bread.

The city buzzed with activity as people hurriedly made their way through the narrow streets. The aroma of freshly baked bread floated through the air, tantalizing my senses and evoking memories of our Lord's last supper. Excitement mingled with reverence coursed through my veins, for this gathering held a special significance to us all.

We arrived at the Gathering Place, a humble yet hallowed space where believers gathered to share in the Communion of the Body and Blood of Christ. As we entered, I was greeted by familiar faces and warm smiles. I introduced Peter to Dionysius, a man whose faith burned with a fervor unmatched, stood tall with an unwavering devotion in his eyes. Adriana and Luciana, sisters in the faith, radiated a gentle joy as they embraced one another, their bond a testament to the unity of the early Church.

Then we saw Martin and Antonius chatting at the other end of the hall with a new group of Ephesians eager to learn more about Jesus and discerning their role as followers of the Christ. I introduced Peter to them. First was Martin, a man known for his unwavering love for others, extended a hand of friendship towards all who crossed his path and was happy to meet Peter. Antonius, whom Peter had met during his time preaching in Tarsus, embraced each other as brothers. Antonius was a steadfast pillar of strength, yet his quiet resolve inspiring those around him. Peter seemed to have made quite an impression on this group, as they enthusiastically engaged in discussions about Jesus and what drew Peter to Him.

As the hour approached, several of us gathered around the table adorned with the simple elements: bread and wine. The air was charged with anticipation and reverence, for in this sacred moment, we experienced a profound connection to our Lord and Savior. The rest of the group sat on benches set so all could see.

We started with a song, giving praise to the Lord for gathering us all together. Then Martin got up and opened the scroll and said "the first reading is from Second Chronicles chapter 5 - The trumpeters and musicians joined in unison to give praise and thanks to the Lord. Accompanied by trumpets, cymbals, and other instruments, the singers raised their voices in praise to the Lord and sang: 'He is good; his love endures forever.' Then the temple of the Lord was filled with the cloud. The Word of the Lord".

We all responded "Thanks be to God in the highest".

Then, Dionysius rose from his place and with open hands pointing toward the heavens, said "Let us all sing Psalm 95 – 'Oh come, let us sing to the Lord; let us make a joyful noise to the rock of our salvation! Let us come into his presence with thanksgiving; let us make a joyful noise to him with songs of praise!"

I stood up and asked for everyone to stand in reverence for what I was about to say. I started, "God loved the world so much He gave His one and only Son! Whoever believes in him will not perish but have eternal life. For God did not send his Son into the world to condemn the world, but to save the world through His suffering and Death. All who believes in Him is not condemned, but whoever does not believe stands condemned already because they have not believed in the name of God's one and only Son. Light has come into the world, but people loved darkness instead of light because their deeds were evil. Everyone who does evil hates the light, and will not come into the light for fear that their deeds will become exposed. But whoever lives by the truth comes into the light, so that it may be seen plainly that what they have done has been done in the sight of God."

I continued, "please be seated. The first verse read by Martin describes a momentous occasion in the history of Israel when the Ark of the Covenant was brought into the newly built temple in Jerusalem. The people, including the priests and musicians, gathered together to offer praise and thanks to the Lord. They celebrated His goodness and proclaimed His enduring love. Then, the psalm read by Dionysius is a favorite of mine – it reminds us that gathering together to praise God is not only an act of reverence but also an opportunity to express gratitude for His saving grace. It encourages believers to approach God's presence with joy, embracing the privilege of worshiping Him as a community. By joining together in song and thanksgiving, we are reminded of the blessings we have received and the greatness of our

God. It is a call to celebrate His faithfulness, goodness, and salvation as a unified body of believers."

"Then the reading I shared with you, Words directly from Jesus, proclaims the reason He was sent – to free us from darkness so we can walk in the light! God the Father created each and every one of us. He created us to love us. From the time of the Garden, the evil one has placed each of us in bondage – chains of Adam and Eve to live in darkness. Many have chosen to live in that darkness, disobeying every commandment given to Moses on the mountain. It is our duty as followers of Jesus to stay in the light He provides for us and to reach deep into the darkness and pull our family and friends into the light – to show them how good it is to live in the light and follow the Lord", I proclaimed as I returned to recline at the table.

Then with trembling hands, Peter blessed and broke the bread, an act that echoed the breaking of Christ's body on the cross. The aroma of the fresh baked unleavened bread mingled with the scent of incense, creating a heady atmosphere that filled our senses. We partook of the bread, sharing in the spiritual nourishment, mindful of the sacrifice that had been made for us.

As we sipped from the cup, the rich taste of its contents filled our mouths, reminding us of the blood shed for our redemption. In that intimate moment, our hearts were knit together, bound by a shared faith and a deep love for our Lord.

In the Gathering Place, amidst the fellowship of about 50 believers, the mundane world melted away, and we were transported to a realm where the divine intersected with the earthly. It was a glimpse of heaven, a foretaste of the eternal feast yet to come.

Before I left with Mary, Luciana and Adriana approached me and said that they loved how I shared with them about Jesus and why He came to save us. Luciana said "we love to write and it would be an honor to capture your stories on parchment". Mary looked upward and mouthed "Thank you". God seems to work in mysterious ways!

As the sun dipped below the horizon, casting its final blush of color upon the city, we departed the Gathering Place with hearts aflame. The breaking of the bread had nourished not only our bodies but also our souls, leaving an indelible mark that would guide us on our journey of faith until we would gather again, united in our love for Christ and one another.

Fervent Zeal, Guided Grace

In our bustling city of Ephesus, a Jew named Apollos, a native of Alexandria arrived. We heard that he carried with him a fervent zeal for the Lord, having been instructed in the ways of the Lord. With great passion, he fearlessly proclaimed the truth about Jesus, although his understanding was limited to the baptism of John the Baptist. We wondered if we had another Simon Magus of Samaria who had practiced sorcery and amazed the people with his magical abilities, even claiming to possess divine power.

Eager to share his message, Apollos took to the synagogue across town, speaking with boldness and conviction. We sent Priscilla and Aquila from Corinth, devoted disciples of Christ, to hear him speak. His eloquence and deep knowledge of the Scriptures amazed them. Recognizing the fervor and potential in Apollos, they lovingly took him aside and expounded to him the Way of God.

Priscilla and Aquila invited Apollos to the Gathering Place to meet Peter, Paul, Mary and me. Although we had a big open field and a well rich in fresh, clean water, we didn't have adequate lodging for our growing community. When they arrived with Apollos, we discussed our dilemma. We never knew this, because we concentrated on vetting their faith understanding, but they said they were professional tent makers! We can teach two things at once, building a home for people to sleep in and building a home for Jesus to live in!

Several days later, Paul arrived in Ephesus to see Peter. He seemed quite surprised that Mary and I had made our way there as well. There was great anticipation as we assembled at Gathering Place, a sacred refuge where the devoted disciples of Christ in Ephesus convened for the breaking of the bread. We have been so blessed to have Tyrannus donate this space for us to gather, pray and fellowship.

The room exuded a sense of reverence, bathed in the warm glow of flickering candles. Shadows danced upon the walls, casting a ghostly veil over the weathered surfaces. As we entered, our eyes met the familiar faces of Dionysius, Adriana, Luciana, Martin, and Antonius, and many other dear companions in the faith. They had been very active disciples with us in Ephesus.

Amidst the gathering, Priscilla and Aquila, ever-dedicated to the spread of the Good News, stood alongside Apollos, his zeal for the Lord burning bright like a blazing sun. Paul, Peter, Mary and I filed in and stood next to Apollos. Tyrannus also came in and stood next to me.

As we congregated around the simple wooden table, adorned with fragrant unleavened bread and a cup of wine, a hushed solemnity settled over the room. With reverence and gratitude, we began with singing and reading of Scriptures and one of the accounts of Jesus' life. Peter gave a wonderful reflection on the scripture readings, emphasizing the suffering and persecution faced by believers. He encouraged us to endure and remain faithful. He draws from the Old Testament, particularly the example of the suffering servant in Isaiah, to illustrate the redemptive value of suffering and the hope that lies in Christ's sacrifice.

He also emphasized the concept of holiness and righteous living, drawing from Leviticus and other Old Testament passages that highlight the importance of living a life set apart for God. He emphasized the call to be holy and referenced the Levitical law to emphasize the transformative power of God's grace in the lives of believers.

Additionally, Peter cited the Psalms 34 and Psalm 118 which were sung earlier, to illustrate the themes of praise, trust, and the deliverance of God. He drew on the experiences of figures like David and the prophets to encourage believers to find hope and strength in God during times of trial and uncertainty.

Then, in that sacred moment, surrounded by those dear to our hearts, I sensed the presence of the Holy Spirit descending upon us like a gentle dove. The room seemed to vibrate with a divine harmony, as if heaven itself had brushed against our mortal realm. Our hearts swelled with joy, and tears of gratitude streamed down our weathered cheeks.

Within the fellowship of that intimate gathering, as we shared the consecrated bread and wine, we were united as one body, bound together by the love of our Savior. The breaking of the bread became a tangible expression of our shared devotion, a sacrament that transcended time and space.

As twilight embraced the city of Ephesus, painting the sky with hues of purple and gold, we departed Tyrannus' Gathering Place, carrying within us the flame of our shared faith. The echoes of prayers, laughter, and hymns lingered in the air, a testament to the enduring power of Christ's love within the hearts of His disciples in Ephesus.

Over the next days, Apollos was not only enlightened by Priscilla and Aquila's coaching but also empowered to continue his ministry with renewed vigor. The encounter between Apollos and this faithful couple would prove to be a significant moment in the history of the early Church, as it paved the way for the expansion of the Good News and the strengthening of believers in various regions.

Gifted with both knowledge and oratory skills and the coaching of Aquila and Priscilla, Apollos became an influential figure, igniting faith and conviction in the hearts of many who met with him out by the Mosaic. Paul witnessed his passionate proclamation of the truth and how it captivated audiences and solidified the belief of those who had found redemption in Christ.

Enlightened by the wisdom and insights shared by Priscilla and Aquila, Paul asked Apollos if he would like to journey further with him, desiring to cross into Achaia, specifically the city of Corinth. All of us brothers and sisters in Ephesus, recognizing his dedication and calling, provided him with every encouragement and support to travel on with Paul. They even penned a letter for Paul to carry to the disciples in Corinth, requesting that they warmly receive and embrace Apollos.

Upon their arrival in Corinth, Apollos became a mighty pillar of strength for those who had come to believe in Jesus through the transformative power of grace. Armed with powerful arguments and the Scriptures, he fearlessly engaged in public debates with the Jews, using the words of the prophets to conclusively demonstrate that Jesus is indeed the long-awaited Messiah, the Christ.

As Apollos embarked on this next chapter of his journey, his impact resonated far beyond the walls of the synagogues of Corinth and reached the hearts of countless souls yearning for the truth. His compelling arguments and unshakable faith would leave an indelible mark on the early Christian movement, fortifying the foundations of the growing Church.

Paul Hit's a Raw Nerve

While I preached at the Gathering Place with Dionysius and Adriana, Paul continued to preach with Luciana and Martin in the Synagogue across town, and Antonius preached generally at the Mosaic area. We all placed our hands on those who spoke the name of the Lord Jesus and the Holy Spirit can upon them. Many spoke in tongues and prophesied.

Paul was being especially effective at converting large numbers of Ephesians and people from the surrounding towns to turn away from Greek gods. Paul told me, "the Lord has worked wonders thru my tongue and He has headed so many of their afflictions through my hands. Even rags made from my old shirts have been brought to the sick and healed when touched to their body". He continued, "the Jewish leaders have forbidden me to return to their Synagogue to preach The Way."

I told Paul "I think you should let them calm down. The Sadducees and Pharisees in Jerusalem and Judea did the same thing to Jesus and His followers, as you know. But part of God the Father's Plan was to allow Jesus to die a sacrificial death for our sins. Our premature death would only cut short the mission of spreading the Word of Jesus and converting pagans and jews."

Paul said, "So should I leave and if so, where should I go?"

I responded, "Paul, please don't leave yet. I need you to help me maintain the converts here and to strengthen their ability to evangelize themselves. Please help me at the Gathering Place. No one seems to bother us there".

Paul agreed and said, "I also need to write a letter to support those who are in Galatia, especially in the areas around Gordion, Ankyra and Pessinus, so I can do a lot from 'behind the scenes'". He continued "I need to condemn the influence of certain Jewish Christian teachers who have been advocating for circumcision and adherence to the Jewish law as being necessary for salvation. I will defend my own apostleship and the message of grace, asserting that salvation is through faith in Christ alone, not by works of the law."

I told him that this might be a hard sell, reminding him of the strong words we had with Peter about the subject. I told him to make sure he used words of love, not condemnation. I also told him to share his own experience and conversion to reinforce the authority of his message. He should highlight that he did not receive his knowledge of the Good News from human sources but through direct revelation from Jesus Christ.

Paul said that he needs to reinforce that the true children of Abraham are those who have faith, not just those who follow the law. That he needs to emphasize that Jesus Christ's redemptive work fulfills the promise made to Abraham, making all believers, both Jews and Gentiles, heirs to the promise.

Paul also said that "I need to emphasize the freedom that believers have in Christ and warn against returning to a yoke of slavery through sin as well as strict adherence to the law. I will explain that through faith, believers are no longer under the law's condemnation but are justified by Christ's sacrifice. But, of course, I need to urge the Galatians to live according to the Spirit rather than the flesh, contrasting the works of the flesh with the fruit of the Spirit, emphasizing the importance of love, joy, peace, and other godly virtues."

I encouraged Paul to tell them to bear one another's burdens, to do good to all, and to sow to the Spirit. And through the grace of God, not to be swayed by the false teachers' influence.

The next morning, I decided to go for a walk. Adriana and Luciana, entrusted with the weighty task of documenting the profound teachings of Jesus thru me, walked alongside, eager to start. I told them "As you write, may your pen be guided by the Holy Spirit to capture my words and that they may be a powerful witness to the truth of Jesus Christ."

Even though I told them "Jesus Himself said, 'If you love Me, you will keep My commandments'", our love for God must not just be a matter of words, but it must be demonstrated in our actions. We must live lives that are pleasing to God, following in the footsteps of Jesus Christ.

I continued, "And yet, even as we strive to obey God's commandments, we must also remember that we are sinners in need of His grace. None of us are perfect, and we all fall short of the glory of God. But if we confess our sins, He will forgive us and cleanse us from all unrighteousness." Then I told them, "We must never take God's forgiveness for granted, but instead, we must humbly seek His forgiveness and strive to live lives that are pleasing to Him."

"Just as in my time with Jesus, there are those who would seek to lead God's people astray with their false doctrines. We must be on guard against such teachings and test everything against the truth of God's word. We must hold fast to the truth of the Good News, rejecting anything that is not in accordance with it", I explained.

I continued, "In addition, we must also emphasize the importance of love for one another. Jesus Himself said, 'By this all people will know that you are My disciples, if you have love for one another'. We must show love to all people, even those who are difficult to love. We must forgive others as we have been forgiven, and seek to reconcile with those whom we have wronged or who have wronged us."

"We must also encourage one another in the faith, building each other up and spurring one another on to love and good works." I said, continuing "We must not neglect meeting together, but instead, gather together regularly to worship God and fellowship with one another. In doing so, we will be strengthened and encouraged to continue in the faith." We always benefit in graces by our actions.

"And finally, we must remember that our ultimate hope is in Jesus Christ. He is the one who has overcome the world, and He is the one who will one day return to set all things right. In the meantime, we must remain faithful, looking to Him for guidance and direction, and trusting in His promise to be with us always, even to the end of the age."

I said, "My dear Adriana and Luciana, may these words inspire you to write a document that will be a powerful witness to the truth of Jesus Christ. May these words encourage and challenge God's people to live lives that are pleasing to Him, to hold fast to the truth of the Good News, and to love one another as He has loved us. May we all, as His disciples, continue to follow in His footsteps, sharing the good news of salvation with all who will listen, and bringing hope and healing to a world in need."

We must always communicate with boldness and conviction, knowing that the Holy Spirit will guide and empower us every step of the way. May our words be a beacon of truth and light in a world that is darkened by sin and confusion. And may all who read this document you are writing for me be inspired to live lives that are pleasing to God, filled with love, joy, and peace.

Together, we continued to navigate the bustling streets of Ephesus, carrying the light of Christ into the darkest corners of the city. Guided by the Holy Spirit, we shared the Good News with those hungering for truth, extending a hand of compassion and a message of hope.

In the marketplace, the temples, and the homes of Ephesus, the teachings of Jesus spread like wildfire. The wisdom and authority we passed down resonated in the words and actions of those in our community. Lives were transformed, hearts were awakened, and the kingdom of darkness trembled in the face of the advancing Kingdom of God. Under the watchful gaze of Priscilla and Aquila, faithful stewards of God's truth, we nurtured a community of believers, providing support, discipleship, and encouragement.

As the days turned into weeks and the weeks into months, the fellowship we shared deepened, strengthened by the bonds forged in service to the risen Lord. Together, we navigated trials and persecution, rejoicing in the privilege of suffering for the sake of the Good News.

And in the breaking of the bread, we found sustenance not only for our physical bodies but for our spirits, nourished by the eternal truths embodied in the body and blood of Christ. It was a sacred act, a symbol of our unity and communion with one another and with our Lord.

In Ephesus, amidst the vibrant community of believers, our love for one another grew, fueled by the love that flowed from the heart of Jesus. The echoes of our shared worship, prayers, and teachings reverberated through the city, drawing more souls to the saving grace of our Savior.

The legacy of our time in Ephesus would endure, like a beacon of light in a world shrouded in darkness. We were privileged to witness the transformative power of Christ's love firsthand, as lives were redeemed, and a fledgling church emerged, ready to face the challenges and triumphs that lay ahead.

Paul converted large numbers of people here in Ephesus and in practically the whole province of Asia. He began to preach that gods made by human hands are not gods at all. Demetrius, a skilled silversmith who specialized in crafting silver shrines for Diana, played a significant role in generating substantial business for his fellow craftsmen. He gathered these artisans and others in related trades, addressing them with concern. "Gentlemen," he began, "you are well aware of how our prosperity hinges on this specific trade. If you observe and listen, you will also recognize that this man named Paul has been remarkably successful in Ephesus and even throughout the province of Asia, persuading a considerable number of individuals to abandon their belief in gods crafted by human hands. Now, the danger we face is twofold: not only might our profession fall into disrepute, but also the revered temple of the great goddess Diana could lose its esteemed status. There is an additional peril that her true majesty might be diminished, despite the fact that she is worshipped by all of Asia and indeed the entire world!"

Upon hearing this, the crowd became fiercely angry and cried out, "Diana of the Ephesians is magnificent!"

Soon, the entire city was in chaos, as the people, acting together, stormed into the Gathering Place, dragging along Gaius and Aristarchus, Macedonians who were companions of Paul. Although Paul himself desired to enter the crowd, we prevented him from doing so. Furthermore, some influential officials, who were friendly with Paul, sent word, imploring him not to risk his safety by appearing in the Gathering Place.

Meanwhile, the multitude shouted conflicting statements, and the entire gathering was in disarray, as most of them were unsure why they had gathered in the first place! At that moment, a man named Alexander, put forward by the Jews, was pushed to the forefront of the crowd. He gestured with his hand, attempting to deliver a speech in defense, but as soon as the crowd realized he was a Jew and there to stir up trouble, they collectively shouted for approximately two hours, "Diana of the Ephesians is magnificent!"

Mary thanks Paul for bringing up the false god issue and he served the purpose of getting people to think about what they were putting their faith into. It also was very interesting to see the dynamics of the crowd – How there were the silversmiths who seemed to be the ones inciting violence, not because of Paul speaking against their gods, but because their money-making abilities would diminish. Then there were the jews who were against the teachings of Jesus, and finally the average Ephesian who really was just proud of their city's historical god. Mary suggested that Paul travel back to Judea, that three years in one location was probably too much for him.

The next day, Paul, Gaius and Aristarchus set sail to return to Caesarea and then travelled on foot on to Jerusalem.

The Debate

It was a beautiful morning when Mother Mary suggested that I go out to the Mosaic and share the Good News with those who were willing to lend an ear. As a disciple of Jesus, I eagerly embraced the opportunity. Little did I know that this encounter would be with followers of Artemis, but I trusted that it was part of God's plan.

With a warm greeting, I introduced myself as John, one of the closest apostles to Jesus. I stood before them with a message of hope and transformation, fully aware of their devotion was most likely to Artemis. Believing the significance Artemis held in their lives, I felt compelled to explain how the teachings of Jesus offered a deeper understanding of divine truth and a pathway to eternal life. I hoped they would be open to engaging in a friendly discussion about these profound differences.

One of the followers of Artemis, respectful yet curious, greeted me back. They expressed their willingness to listen, but also made it clear that Artemis held a position of high esteem in their hearts. They wondered how Jesus' message could possibly relate to their deep devotion to Artemis.

Grateful for their openness, I took a moment to collect my thoughts. With gentleness and respect, I explained that Jesus' message was not about merely adding Him to their pantheon of deities. Instead, it was about discovering the ultimate truth and finding true fulfillment in a personal relationship with the one true God. While Artemis represented certain aspects of the divine, I shared that Jesus offered a direct communion with the Creator Himself—a relationship that went beyond what they had experienced before.

Another follower of Artemis, their eyes filled with curiosity, asked a crucial question. They wanted to know how we could be sure that Jesus' claims were true and not just another belief system.

Drawing from my own personal experiences as one who walked and talked with Jesus, I assured them that this was not mere speculation or blind faith. Jesus' life and teachings were marked by undeniable evidence. He performed astonishing miracles that demonstrated His divine power and authority over creation. The blind received sight, the lame walked, and even the dead were raised back to life. Moreover, His resurrection after His crucifixion stood as the most powerful testament to His divine nature. I spoke of the countless eyewitnesses who had seen Him alive after His death—individuals who had their lives transformed by encountering the risen Christ. Their unwavering faith and commitment to Jesus were a testament to the truth of His message, standing strong even in the face of persecution.

As the discussion unfolded, I earnestly prayed that the Holy Spirit would touch their hearts and open their minds to the profound truth found in Jesus' teachings.

"John, we appreciate your perspective. By the way, my name is Alexandros, she is Maria and he is Andreas. Please recognize that Artemis has been our guiding light for generations. Her temple in Ephesus is renowned, attracting worshippers from far and wide. How can we turn away from our deeply ingrained traditions and embrace this new path you speak of?"

I said, "I understand the deep connection and reverence you have for Artemis, a deity that has guided your lives for generations. The temple in Ephesus stands as a testament to the significance she holds in Ephesus. However, embracing the teachings of Jesus does require a departure from the values of Artemis. It is a call to redirect our devotion and align ourselves with the truth and love found in Christ. While I am a follower of Jesus, I believe there are certain values associated with Artemis that align with the teachings of Jesus. Can I try to explain?"

Andreas said, "Thank you, John. We are curious to hear more about this connection between Artemis and Jesus' teachings."

I explained, "Artemis was revered as a goddess of fertility, protector of women, and guardian of the natural world. These values echo some aspects of Jesus' teachings. Jesus emphasizes the importance of caring for one another, particularly the marginalized and vulnerable. He taught us to treat women with respect, dignity, and equality, recognizing their inherent worth. In this sense, we can see a synergy between the values of Artemis and the teachings of Jesus in their shared emphasis on protecting and nurturing life."

Maria spoke up, "That's an interesting perspective, John. We have always held Artemis in high regard for her connection to women's well-being. How else do you see the values of Artemis aligning with Jesus' teachings?"

"Another value associated with Artemis is her role as a guardian of the natural world.", I said. "She was revered as the goddess of the wilderness, protecting wildlife and the environment. Similarly, Jesus teaches us to be good stewards of God's creation. He emphasizes our responsibility to care for the Earth and its creatures, recognizing that all of creation reflects the beauty and goodness of God. In this regard, the values of Artemis and Jesus converge in their shared concern for the preservation and nurturing of the natural world."

Alexandros said, "I've always admired Artemis' connection to the wilderness. It's intriguing to think of how Jesus' teachings align with that value. Are there any other parallels between Artemis and Jesus' teachings?"

I explained, "Absolutely, Alexandros. Another parallel lies in the idea of protection. Artemis was seen as a guardian and protector, particularly for those in need. Jesus, too, taught us to protect the weak, stand up for justice, and defend the rights of the oppressed. He showed compassion and mercy to the outcasts and challenged social injustices of His time. This shared emphasis on protection and advocacy for the vulnerable further highlights the synergy between the values associated with Artemis and the teachings of Jesus.

"Thank you, John", Andreas said, "for shedding light on these connections. It's fascinating to see how there can be common ground between Artemis' values and Jesus' teachings. How can we incorporate these values into our lives if we were followers of Jesus?"

"As a follower of Jesus, I can appreciate the values associated with Artemis. We can draw inspiration from Artemis' dedication to protecting life, nurturing the vulnerable, and respecting the natural world. These and other reasons, God the Father send Jesus, His Only Son to us to share in the Father's love, compassion, and stewardship. In doing so, Jesus shows not just His own Love and Mercy but also the Father's. Hundreds of thousands of people in Jerusalem up past the Galilee have witnessed that love and mercy from the Father thru the works of the Son, Jesus.", I related.

Maria said, "Thank you, John, for sharing these insights. It's refreshing to see the interconnectedness of different beliefs and how they can converge in meaningful ways that we can relate to. The part that I have a hard time with is that Jesus came to live among us. This is very foreign to our way of thinking."

I said, "You're most welcome, Maria. Embracing the values of Artemis and Jesus can lead us to a deeper understanding of God's truth and broaden our appreciation for the diverse expressions of faith. May your journey be filled with love, understanding, and as you build upon these values you will have a better understanding of who Jesus is. I am watching over Jesus' mother here in Ephesus. Her name is Mary. That's another thing you have in common, your names Maria!" Then I told them is She was feeling up to it, I would ask Her to join me tomorrow.

Andreas said, "Our devotion to Artemis gives us a sense of identity and community. Would following Jesus mean leaving that behind?

I said, "I appreciate the importance of identity and community in your lives. Following Jesus does involve leaving behind the worship of Artemis, but it also opens the door to a new and eternal community of believers. In this community, united by the love of Christ, you will find a deep sense of identity rooted in being children of God. You will discover a fellowship that surpasses any earthly bonds, where love, support, and a shared purpose bring you closer to one another and to God."

Alexandros said, "We appreciate your perspective, John. But how do we reconcile our rituals and practices with the teachings of Jesus?"

I told them, "It is a valid question to consider. Embracing Jesus' message requires a transformation of heart and a shift in focus toward worshiping the one true God. The essence of true worship lies in loving God with all our hearts and loving our neighbors as ourselves. It means leaving behind practices that may contradict His teachings and instead embracing a life of love, righteousness, and service to others."

Alexandros said that this all was a lot to take in, but much of it seems to be understandable. Beliefs in multiple gods, whom no one has ever seen certainly casts doubts in the beliefs that they are real. He continued that it will be good to speak with Mary to get some answers to their questions.

I said, "I am excited that you are considering this transformative journey toward Jesus. Finding out how easy it is to seek and find forgiveness for past actions and commit to a life guided by His teachings of love, compassion, and forgiveness will allow you a freedom you never thought possible! You'll be able to engage with other believers, study His words, and allow the Holy Spirit to guide you on this transformative path. Remember, it is a lifelong journey of growth, faith, and spiritual fulfillment."

They all got up and said how much they look forward to chatting with Mary as well as with me again. With that, they walked toward the Theater and appeared to be in deep debate with one another as they disappeared into the distance.

As the sun cast its warm glow over the bustling city of Ephesus, I found myself standing amidst the mosaic, a gathering place that teemed with the energy of curious souls seeking wisdom and meaning. Mother Mary came with me, but I had to promise to get her home before the hot sun reached it's pinnacle. It was here, at the mosaic yesterday, amidst the intricate patterns that adorned the ground, that I encountered my new friends, Andreas, Maria, and Alexandros. They approached again today from the direction of the Theater, their faces filled with a mixture of intrigue and longing, as if they carried the weight of unspoken questions within their hearts.

"John," Andreas began, his voice crackled with anticipation, "we have heard stories of your close relationship with Jesus, the Son of God. But today, we are particularly drawn to the presence of Mary, the blessed mother who witnessed the unfolding of God's plan. We yearn to understand her experiences and why we should put our trust in Jesus' teachings. Hi Mary, I am Andreas, this is Maria and this is Alexandro"

I turned my gaze toward Mary, whose gentle eyes radiated a profound sense of love and wisdom. She stood there, a pillar of strength, her presence an embodiment of the miraculous and the divine. The years had etched lines upon her face, testament to the joys and sorrows she had carried as the mother of our beloved Savior.

With a gentle nod, Mary acknowledged their yearning for knowledge and understanding. "Dear friends, I am honored to share my experiences and the teachings of my precious son, Jesus. His life was not simply a sequence of miracles and wonders; it was a profound revelation of God's love and the redemption that is available to all."

They gathered closer, spirits open and receptive to the truths that were about to unfold. The mosaic beneath their feet seemed to mirror the intricacies of their own journey of beliefs, each piece representing a unique story woven into the grand tapestry of human existence.

Maria began, directing my words to Mary, "as a mother, I believe you possess a unique perspective on the life and teachings of your special son, Jesus. Could you share with us a glimpse into your journey and the reasons why we should put our trust in Him?"

A soft smile graced Mary's lips, her voice carrying a depth that could only be born from a wellspring of profound love. "Andreas, Maria, and Alexandros, my heart overflows with joy to see your eagerness to understand. An angel from Heaven appeared to me as a young teenager and said that I had found favor with God and He wanted me to remain a virgin, but to give birth to the Messiah. It came as quite a surprise, but I said yes. When I held my son in my arms, I absolutely knew He was no ordinary child. The divine presence within Him was undeniable, and as He grew, it became more and more evident that His purpose was to illuminate the path to salvation."

She paused, her eyes gazing into the distance, as if revisiting memories etched within her soul. "Jesus lived a life of compassion and selflessness. His teachings were grounded in love, forgiveness, and the redemption of all humanity. He walked among us, healing the sick, comforting the broken-hearted, and embracing the outcasts. Through His life, He exemplified the very essence of God's unconditional love."

I glanced at my friends, their expressions a mixture of wonder and contemplation. It was as if a veil had been lifted, revealing the profound truth that lay before us.

"Mary," Alexandros inquired with a touch of hesitancy, "how can we be certain that Jesus' teachings are indeed the path to salvation? In a world filled with different beliefs and ideologies, how do we know that we can trust Him?"

Mary's eyes sparkled with warmth and certainty, her voice resonating with unwavering conviction. "My dear Alexandros, doubt is a natural part of our human journey, but faith allows us to transcend uncertainty. Throughout Jesus' ministry, He performed miracles that surpassed human comprehension. He restored sight to the blind, walked upon water, and even conquered death itself. But His most profound miracle was the transformation He ignited within the hearts of those who encountered.

As Mary spoke, her words were interwoven with the wisdom that only the mother of the Messiah could possess. "Love God the best you can," she said, her voice filled with tenderness. "In your pursuit of truth and understanding, remember that God's love is boundless and everlasting. He longs for a relationship with each one of you and will never abandon you."

I sensed the yearning in their hearts, added, "The teachings of Jesus go beyond mere intellectual comprehension. They require a personal, transformative encounter with the Holy Spirit. When you open your hearts to God, the Holy Spirit dwells within you, guiding your steps and illuminating the path of righteousness."

Mary chimed in, saying "This may be a bit too much to understand today, but my Son Jesus is one Person in the Holy Trinity. They are one God in three Persons – God the Father, God the Son, and God the Holy Spirit"

I let that sink in a bit then said "we can chat about that in the days to come. It is difficult for any of us, but that is why we call it faith. Some things are too difficult for our human brains to figure out. But There is only one God, made up in three persons. They existed from the beginning of time and will exist until the end of time. Before as well as after the existence of the earth, the sun and all the stars of the sky."

Andreas, his eyes gleaming with this newfound insight, questioned, "But in a world filled with distractions and temptations, how do we remain steadfast in our commitment to follow Jesus?"

Mary smiled, her gaze steady and unwavering. "We are in this world, but not of this world," she said, her words carrying a sense of reassurance. "Jesus understood the trials and tribulations of the world, yet He triumphed over them. Through Him, we find the strength to navigate the challenges of our earthly existence, for His teachings offer us a compass to steer our souls toward eternal life."

Maria, her heart filled with gratitude, spoke softly, "Mary, your words touch the depths of our souls. We long to experience the transformation and love that you and John have encountered. How do we take the next step? How do we embrace Jesus and His teachings fully?"

Mary extended her hands, her voice resolute yet gentle. "Embrace the gift of faith," she said. "Trust in the love of God and surrender your lives to Him. Seek His guidance through prayer and meditation. Immerse yourselves in the teachings of Jesus, for in them you will find the keys to abundant life. Let the Holy Spirit work within you, molding your hearts and renewing your minds. And remember, my dear friends, that this journey is not one you walk alone. You have each other, the community of believers, and the unending love of God to support you along the way."

As the words settled within their souls, a sense of peace and purpose enveloped them. The mosaic beneath their feet seemed to shimmer with newfound meaning, reflecting the intricate design of our interconnected lives.

Andreas, Maria, and Alexandros, now filled with a profound sense of hope, took Mary's hands in theirs. They knew that their journey had just begun, that they would face challenges and uncertainties, but they also knew that they had been entrusted with a precious truth.

With Mother Mary and me by their side, they were ready to embarked on a transformative path, embracing Jesus' teachings and the love that transcended time and space. I brought the jug filled with water, I blessed it and baptized them in the name of the Father, the Son and the Holy Spirit. Then I laid my hands upon each of their heads and prayed that they receive the gifts of the Holy Spirit. They carried within their hearts the assurance that, in this world, they would navigate with the strength of their new faith and the guiding presence of the Holy Spirit. For they had learned that love for God, the knowledge of His unwavering love for them, and the embrace of their divine purpose were the compass that would lead them toward a life of eternal significance.

They all were so grateful for our patience and the insight we had shared. They said that it all started with an invitation to follow Him and they looked forward to extending that invitation to all they encountered.

I told them to come and break bread with us at the Gathering Place and they, too, would receive graces that come from receiving the Body and Blood of Jesus. May God bless you for seeking the truth.

How Could I Ask for More

As Mother Mary and I walked back to the house, she talked about how blessed she felt to help share the Good News of her Son. But she struggled so much as she took each step. I told her I wanted to carry her, but she said that she will never be carried until her Son carried her into Heaven. She said her Son struggled all the way to Calvary, she would make it the couple blocks back to the house.

When we arrived, I got her to sit while I poured her an ice-cold cup of water fresh from the well. She then said she was tired and wanted to lay down for a nap.

While she did so, I went to the store for some supplies for the week ahead. When I returned, Mother Mary was awake. After I put the supplies away, I asked her if I could get her anything. She replied that the mid-day sun wasn't so hot and there was a nice breeze from the sea. She asked if I could help her to the garden. Her legs seemed quite weak, but she insisted again to walk.

She said, "my dear John, as we strolled through this beautiful garden, I was reminded of the importance of growth and nurture in the life of a believer. Just as these flowers require care and attention to bloom and flourish, so too must we nurture our faith and walk in the truth of the Good News.

"As we enjoy the fragrant scents and vibrant colors around us, I am reminded of the beauty of love and the importance of walking in obedience to God's commands. It is by our love for one another that the world will know that we are His disciples, and it is by walking in obedience to His commands that we show our love for Him."

"But my dear John," she continued, "I must also caution you of the dangers of false teachers. Just as these beautiful flowers can hide thorns and prickly vines, so too can false teachers deceive and harm those who are not watchful. They will try to infiltrate the church, spreading lies and false teachings that lead to bondage rather than freedom. Remember none of us thought that any within our group would betray Jesus"

"Therefore, I urge you to be vigilant and watchful, to guard against these deceivers and to warn your fellow believers. Do not let them into your homes or show them hospitality, for by doing so, you are enabling their deception. Judas was not evil himself, but he allowed evil to cloud his judgement of right and wrong. There are serious consequences to opening an ear to the evil one and his evil helpers", She said.

"I will not let the fear of false teachers rob me and any of His followers of the joy and freedom that we have in Christ." I said, "By the power of the Holy Spirit, we can discern the truth and overcome the lies of the enemy. Let us continue to walk in love and obedience to God's commands, and let our words and actions be a witness to the truth of the Good News".

She went on to tell me to teach with urgency, for the time is short and the enemy is relentless. Teach with boldness, knowing that the truth you proclaim from Jesus will set people free. And teach with love, for it is by love that we overcome all things.

She continued to say "My son, do not underestimate the power of your words. You have been called to be a voice for the truth in a world full of lies. You have been entrusted with the message of salvation that has the power to transform lives and set people free. Let your words be a lamp that guides the people of God to the truth of His Good News. Let your words be a shield that protects them from the schemes of the enemy. And let your words be a beacon of hope that leads them to the love and salvation of our Lord Jesus Christ."

"Just as this bench provides a place of rest and comfort, so too does fellowship with like-minded believers provide a sense of peace and joy in our lives. It is in this fellowship that we can encourage and strengthen one another in our faith, and it is through this unity that we show the world the love of Christ."

But my dear John she said, "let us not be deceived into thinking that all fellowship is beneficial. Just as this bench could become weak and unstable if not properly maintained, so too can fellowship with the followers of Jesus become weak and unstable if we allow false teachings and sinful behavior to go unchecked."

"Therefore, I urge you to remain steadfast in the truth of the Good News and to hold fast to the teachings that you have received. Do not be swayed by those who would try to lead you astray, but rather stand firm in your faith and encourage your fellow believers to do the same. Remember, that our joy is made complete when we walk in obedience to God's commands. Let us continue to love one another and walk in the truth, so that our fellowship may be a source of joy and encouragement to all who join us."

Then she turned directly into my eyes and said, "John, in all these years since the cross, I have loved being with you so much. Jesus often told me that He had a special brotherly love for you and I can honestly say I understand why He said you were His Beloved Apostle – you really are! The other folks all love and were loved, but you are special and I am so glad to call you my son.

She then sat back on the bench and said "Today is a beautiful day. The flowers smell wonderful and the birds are singing and I am with my adopted son, whom Jesus Loved. How could I ask for more?" She took a deep breath, as if she wanted to smell the flowers, but she closed her eyes and exhaled. Her entire body started to float off the bench into the air. I saw the few fluffy clouds in the sky split open and she floated between them. They moved together once again.

I began to cry, as she has been such a large part of my life. Then I heard angels singing. I then knew why she said "How could I ask for more". I said, "Lord Jesus, thank you. Thank you for the gift of being with you three years and so many more with your mom – no, our mom!"

Changes

With a renewed sense of mission importance I went out to the Gathering Place to speak of the importance of hospitality and support for those who were called to preach the Good News to the pagans and the communities previously preached to by the others. When I arrived, I was surprised to see my good friends Dionysis, Andriana and Luciana had returned from their year long mission to the Galatian towns of Gordion, Ankyra and Pernius.

They said that Martin and Antonius had noticed how few people traveling westward through Galatia know the Good News of Jesus, so they decided to travel East toward areas of northern Cappadocia to begin spreading the Word.

I was reminded of the time when I was visited by some missionaries who were on their way to preach the Good News in a distant land. They were weary and in need of rest, and how I had opened my home to them, providing them with food and shelter. I knew that their journey would be long and difficult, and I wanted to do everything in my power to give them the support and help they on their way.

And it is this same spirit of hospitality and support that I must urge all here to show that support to those who are called to preach the Good News as they pass thru. Having Dionysis, Andriana and Luciana here shows the great power of the Holy Spirit! His timing is always perfect!

As folks started to arrive for the Breaking of the Bread, I introduced them to Dionysis, Andriana and Luciana as our own missionaries to Galatia and beyond. Andreas, Maria and Alexandros were very excited to meet them as I had told them so much about them as I told they about the importance of discipleship not only to our neighbors, but also to venture out to those towns who didn't know of Jesus.

I asked everyone to sit and began to speak, "It is important that we all remember that this work is not about us, but about the glory of God. It is through our support and encouragement of those who are called to travel and preach the Good News that we can play a part in spreading the Word to all corners of the earth."

As they sat in silence, my words seem to linger in their minds. During our fellowship time at the end of our service, they heard firsthand from our own missionaries. The gathering all knew that they had a great responsibility to support the missionaries who were called to preach the Word, so they took a collection and several of them committed to join Dionysis, Andriana and Luciana in their next missionary trip out to join the efforts of Martin and Antonius in Cappadocia. The ever-growing community of believers gathered also knew that they would be relied upon to help them in this important work as time passed.

So many travelers and merchants of all kinds passed through Ephesus, so they would not only need to carry on the mission of Christ to their neighbors, but to the travelers who knew nothing of Jesus as well as disciples on their way to their own mission trips.

Then suddenly, I felt the Holy Spirit tell me that it was time to leave Ephesus. So I spoke up to those gathered and said, "My dear brothers and sisters in Christ. Every day, I see how our efforts bore fruit. Countless lives were transformed by the message of love and redemption they shared. Communities formed, churches were established, and the teachings of Jesus spread like wildfire, illuminating even the darkest corners of the world."

Through my ministry here in Ephesus, I encountered diverse individuals, each with their own unique struggles, strengths and stories. I tried, with the most gentle and compassionate spirit, to became a beacon of love and understanding to all, just as Jesus taught me. I tried to listen intently to those who sought solace, offering words of comfort and encouragement. I was so blessed to have the deep connection with the blessed mother Mary. It allowed me to embrace others with the same unconditional love he had witnessed in her.

I see these qualities in so many of you. Together, we confronted the challenges that laid before us. Yet, in the face of adversity, your resolve only grew stronger. Please remember this - In my darkest hours, I often sought refuge in Mary's presence. Her unwavering faith was a constant source of inspiration and courage. She reminded me of Jesus' words: "Blessed are those who are persecuted because of righteousness, for theirs is the kingdom of heaven." With her gentle strength, she helped me navigate the treacherous path, guiding me back to the unwavering light of Christ's love.

Remember that Jesus came to offer a direct and personal connection with God. He taught that we can approach God as our loving Father, with whom we can have a relationship characterized by intimacy, trust, and love. Through Jesus, we can experience forgiveness of sins, spiritual renewal, and the indwelling of the Holy Spirit, who guides and empowers us on our spiritual journey. Jesus offers a deeper, more intimate spiritual connection than any other rituals or practices can provide.

This community formed by followers of Jesus is truly special. It is a community bound together by love, faith, and a shared commitment to live out Jesus' teachings. It provides support, encouragement, and a sense of belonging. Anyone seeking it can experience an even deeper sense of belonging and purpose among Jesus' followers here and everywhere. Just walk alongside each other, offering love, care, and accountability, while being true to the teaching of Jesus.

Continue to surrender your lives to Jesus, accepting him as your Lord and Savior. It begins with heartfelt repentance, confessing your sins, and placing your faith in Jesus' sacrificial death and resurrection for your salvation. Seek guidance from the Holy Spirit, study the teachings of Jesus, and immerse yourselves in a community of believers who can support and nurture your faith.

Jesus' compassion and love were boundless. He embraced all people, regardless of their backgrounds or social status. He reached out to the marginalized, the outcasts, and the forgotten, offering them acceptance, healing, and hope. His love extended even to those who rejected him. He taught us to love our enemies and to forgive one another, displaying a radical love that transcends human understanding.

Jesus not only taught with words but also lived out his teachings in his actions. He modeled humility by washing the feet of his disciples, showing that true leadership is rooted in service. He demonstrated forgiveness when he forgave those who crucified him, revealing the power of grace to transform hearts. Jesus exemplified compassion by healing the sick, feeding the hungry, and offering solace to the brokenhearted. His life was a testament to the transformative power of love in action.

Our love for God is inseparable from our love for one another. We cannot say that we love God and hate our brothers and sisters in Christ. Instead, we must love one another as He has loved us. This love is not a mere sentiment or emotion, but a sacrificial love that is willing to lay down our lives for one another.

We must remember that our hope is in Jesus Christ. He is the one who has conquered sin and death, and He is the one who will one day return to set all things right. In the meantime, we must remain faithful, looking to Him for guidance and strength, and trusting in His promise to be with us always, even to the end of the age.

Remember always that you are loved and cherished, not only by me but also by your brothers and sisters in Christ. We are all part of the same family, united by our faith in Jesus Christ. Let us encourage one another, pray for one another, and support one another as we journey together on this road of faith.

And above all, let us fix our eyes on Jesus, the author and perfecter of our faith. He is the one who has gone before us, and He is the one who will lead us safely home. Let us trust in Him with all our hearts, knowing that He will never leave us or forsake us. I urge you to emphasize the importance of living lives that are marked by righteousness and holiness.

As I see my mission here is complete, the city and surrounding villages are in good hands with this faith community to continue to build and to thrive. When I leave here, I will travel to Galatia to talk to Antonius in hope that he will accept my invitation to become your leader as the bishop of Ephesus.

Once he accepts this invitation, I will perform a special ceremony, where Antonius will receive the sacrament of Holy Orders in the fullness of the episcopal office of Bishop. Central to this ordination is the laying on of hands which will be done by me placing my hands on his head. This gesture symbolizes the passing on of the apostolic ministry and the imparting of the Holy Spirit for the office of bishop. I will pray over him and present him with various insignia that symbolize his office - a ring, a large pectoral cross, and a crozier. The crozier is a symbol of the bishop's authority and pastoral care over the faithful entrusted to their care. The pastoral staff has its origins in the shepherd's crook, symbolizing the bishop's role as a shepherd of the flock, following the example of Jesus Christ, who we often refer to as the Good Shepherd.

I ask you to accept him with the dignity and respect you have given me once he returns. I celebrate this moment with you. May the grace of our Lord Jesus Christ, the love of God, and the fellowship of the Holy Spirit be with you all as you step into this new chapter of your lives.

Also by John H Brennan

Thru The First Disciple's Eyes
Thru the First Disciple's Eyes
Through the Eyes of the Disciple Jesus Loved

Standalone
Advice From Above
The Rosary Revealed

About the Author

John is a cradle Catholic, the middle child of five, who grew up in upstate New York. Vatican Two saved him from learning Latin the year he trained to be an Altar Server. He attended Catholic School until High School when he transitioned to public school. He received two associates degrees from the local Community College, then started a job in a fortune 500 company as a draftsman. He had met the woman of his dreams and they had the first of their children 9 months after they were married. Six months later, the three headed off to the State University of New York at Buffalo where John studied Mechanical Engineering. By the time John graduated with his BS in Mechanical Engineering, they had their second son and headed back to his hometown to continue his 40 year career and have a third son and finally his daughter. He and his wife now have a son in law, a daughter in law and six beautiful grandchildren. Several events led him to deepen his faith – joining a Catholic Men's Bible Study; attending several Catholic Men's Conferences; attending a Catholic Men's Emmaus Retreat as well as being on several Emmaus Retreat Teams (including giving witness talks); attending daily Mass; Praying the Holy Rosary daily and being an Extraordinary Minister of Holy Communion at Church and Nursing Homes in the area. His engineering job brought him across the USA as well as Mexico, Europe and Asia where he enjoyed creating his own personal Pilgrimages to Holy Sites and sharing the experiences and pictures with family and friends. His retirement ambitions include enjoying his children and grandchildren, continued travel to holy sites around the world and sharing his Catholic faith wherever he can.